I0407001

Perspectives on Embedded Media

Selected Papers from the
U.S. Army War College

Report Documentation Page

Form Approved
OMB No. 0704-0188

Public reporting burden for the collection of information is estimated to average 1 hour per response, including the time for reviewing instructions, searching existing data sources, gathering and maintaining the data needed, and completing and reviewing the collection of information. Send comments regarding this burden estimate or any other aspect of this collection of information, including suggestions for reducing this burden, to Washington Headquarters Services, Directorate for Information Operations and Reports, 1215 Jefferson Davis Highway, Suite 1204, Arlington VA 22202-4302. Respondents should be aware that notwithstanding any other provision of law, no person shall be subject to a penalty for failing to comply with a collection of information if it does not display a currently valid OMB control number.

1. REPORT DATE	2. REPORT TYPE	3. DATES COVERED
NOV 2004	N/A	-

4. TITLE AND SUBTITLE	5a. CONTRACT NUMBER
Perspectives on Embedded Media	5b. GRANT NUMBER
	5c. PROGRAM ELEMENT NUMBER

6. AUTHOR(S)	5d. PROJECT NUMBER
	5e. TASK NUMBER
	5f. WORK UNIT NUMBER

7. PERFORMING ORGANIZATION NAME(S) AND ADDRESS(ES)	8. PERFORMING ORGANIZATION REPORT NUMBER
US Army War College Carlisle, PA 17013	

9. SPONSORING/MONITORING AGENCY NAME(S) AND ADDRESS(ES)	10. SPONSOR/MONITOR'S ACRONYM(S)
	11. SPONSOR/MONITOR'S REPORT NUMBER(S)

12. DISTRIBUTION/AVAILABILITY STATEMENT

Approved for public release, distribution unlimited

13. SUPPLEMENTARY NOTES

14. ABSTRACT

15. SUBJECT TERMS

16. SECURITY CLASSIFICATION OF:			17. LIMITATION OF ABSTRACT	18. NUMBER OF PAGES	19a. NAME OF RESPONSIBLE PERSON
a. REPORT	b. ABSTRACT	c. THIS PAGE	UU	112	
unclassified	unclassified	unclassified			

Standard Form 298 (Rev. 8-98)
Prescribed by ANSI Std Z39-18

Editor

Michael Pasquarett

Associate Editors

John Wheatley

Ritchie Dion

The views expressed in this report are those of the participants and do not necessarily reflect the official policy or position of the United States Army War College, the Department of the Army, The Department of Defense, or any other Department or Agency within the U.S. Government. Further, these views do not reflect uniform agreement among the authors. This report is cleared for public release; distribution is unlimited.

Cover photo courtesy of the *Army Times*

CONTENTS

FOREWORD

During the planning for Operation Iraqi Freedom (OIF) the Department of Defense (DoD) developed an Embedded Media Program that planned for large numbers of embedded reporters throughout military units. Unlike Vietnam in the 1970s, this program resulted in near-real-time television reporting from within Iraq, especially from those reporters embedded with front lines units. The speed with which these reports made it on the air often outpaced the military's communication channels. Although it gave the American citizens an immediate close-up report of what their armed forces were doing, it handicapped media analysts and stateside reporters in their ability to put the raw reporting from the field into a larger context. Conversely, those TV journalists supplying these spectacular reports and engrossing pictures from the front line were also handicapped in that they were reporting in a vacuum, unable themselves to obtain any kind of perspective or context.

On June 6, 2003, at the request of the Army Staff, the U.S Army War College conducted a workshop entitled, "Reporters on the Ground: The Military and the Media's Joint Experience During Operation Iraqi Freedom." This served as both an Army After Action Review and as a forum for a free exchange of experiences, impressions and ideas regarding the Embedded Media Program and its future. Workshop participants featured embedded reporters and the commanders of the units in which they were embedded, unilateral journalists, journalism school academics, and media leadership, along with military academics, public affairs officers, and historians. The workshop reviewed the embedded media experience from three points of view—Tactical, Operational, and Futures—and it provided for open debate on many issues. These issues are included in a Center for Strategic Leadership Issue Paper, which is available online at http://www.carlisle.army.mil/usacsl/IPapers.asp.

As a result of this workshop and of their respective experiences with the media during Operation Iraqi Freedom, five U.S. Army War College students from the class of 2004 made the Embedded Media experience the center of their Strategy Research Project that is an integral part of the U.S. Army War College curriculum, designed to research a topic of importance to the armed forces of the Nation.

These five papers—*Information Operations and the New Threat*, by Lieutenant Colonel Terry R. Ferrell, USA; *The Media and National Security Decision Making*, by Lieutenant Colonel James M. Marye, USA; *Embedded Media: Failed Test, or the Future of Military/Media Relations?* by Lieutenant Colonel Michael J. Oehle, USMC; *Leveraging the Media: The Embedded Media Program in Operation Iraqi Freedom*, by Colonel Glenn T. Starnes, USMC; and *Embedding Success into the Military Media Relationship*, by Commander Jose L. Rodriguez, USNR—have been collected in this volume. With the authors' experiences fresh in their minds, these papers provide a timely and credible review of the successes and failures of the Embedded Media Program; moreover, they provide recommendations and predictions of future difficulties that should be reviewed by anyone with a role to play in the evolving relationship between the media and the military.

Professor Douglas B. Campbell
Director, Center for Strategic Leadership
U.S. Army War College

CHAPTER 1

INFORMATION OPERATIONS AND THE NEW THREAT

Lieutenant Colonel Terry R. Ferrell
United States Army

Since the attacks of 9/11 on the American homeland, the United States has begun an aggressive campaign to defeat terrorists and eradicate terrorism worldwide. President Bush articulated his vision for the Nation as early as September 14, 2001 in a speech at the National Cathedral in Washington, D.C. There he announced the Global War on Terrorism—a policy that would become the major focus for America and other threatened nations: "The United States of America is fighting a war against terrorists of global reach. The enemy is not a single political regime or person or religion or ideology. The enemy is terrorism—premeditated, politically motivated violence perpetrated against innocents."[1] With the fight against terrorism clearly the focus of the Nation's leadership, the Nation committed every element of national power to achieve success in that fight. Not only did the Nation use the elements of national power in the form of diplomatic pressure, economic sanctions and incentives, and military might, but the President also placed a special focus on the use of information operations when he directed that the United States wage a war of ideas to win the battle against international terrorism.[2] This article will analyze the use of information operations in the Global War on Terror and reflect briefly on the lessons from history in determining success in this latest campaign.

THE GLOBAL WAR ON TERROR AND THE NATIONAL SECURITY STRATEGY

Political and economic freedom, peaceful relations with other states, and respect for human dignity are the clearly defined goals of the United States National Security Strategy (NSS).[3] The NSS identifies today's threat to the

1

United States as vastly different from that of the past. The current threat is failing states and "catastrophic technologies in the hands of the embittered few,"[4] a threat known to us as terrorism. The National Security Strategy also identifies eight actions the United States will take to achieve its stated goals. Three of these actions specifically focus on the fight against terrorism:

- strengthening alliances to defeat global terrorism and working to prevent attacks against us and our friends;

- working with others to defuse regional conflicts;

- and preventing our enemies from threatening us, our allies, and our friends, with weapons of mass destruction.[5]

In order to analyze the strategy to support the new U.S. policy, the ends, ways, and means as applied to this policy must be identified. The end in this case is one of the stated actions to achieve the national security goals: "strengthen alliances to defeat global terrorism and work to prevent attacks against us and our friends."[6] The administration understood that the War on Terrorism would not be a war of short duration. Keeping public support behind the long-term campaign would be instrumental to the successful execution of the strategy. That public support would not only be required at home, but also among the major allies in the fight against terrorism. Additionally, the President's war of ideas would be used "to convince other nations and allies that terrorism was unacceptable in any environment."[7] Finally, this war of ideas could be directed at the terrorists themselves, with the United States broadcasting the defeat of one terrorist at a time. A mission so vast would require a specific mechanism to prosecute the new war; thus, the President established the Office of Global Communications through Executive Order 13283 on January 21, 2003.[8] He established the primary role of the new organization as sustaining the will of the American public and keeping the international community abreast of America's pursuit to win the war on terrorism. This new office became the way to achieve our National Security Strategy ends of strengthening alliances.

The primary mission of the Office of Global Communications is to,

> Advise the President, the heads of appropriate offices within the Executive Office of the President, and the heads of executive departments and agencies on utilization of the most effective means for the United States Government to ensure consistency in messages

that will promote the interests of the United States abroad, prevent misunderstanding, build support for and among coalition partners of the United States, and inform international audiences.[9]

The administration's expectation from the establishment of the Office of Global Communication was a closely scrutinized, well-coordinated formulation of themes and messages to broadcast to the world at large. The office would work across the various agencies within the administration to ensure that messages addressed the priorities of the United States and that all agencies spoke in unison. Executive Order 13283 directed the office to "work with the policy and communications offices of agencies in developing a strategy for disseminating truthful, accurate, and effective messages about the United States, its Government and policies, and the American people and culture."[10] On selected issues, when approved by the Department of State and the Assistant to the President for National Security Affairs, the global communications office could directly coordinate with other foreign governments to ensure themes or messages are coordinated and clearly supported within the international framework.[11] Executive Order 13283 defined the "means" for the office to execute the new strategy. This Executive Order directed the office to establish multiple options for delivery and oversight of the messages in support of the National Strategy or general U.S. policies. The office would primarily achieve its objective through the placement of critical strategic communication teams, consisting of members from all the agencies involved in the immediate situation, at critical points that were receiving increased international attention or media attention.[12] The strategic communications team would work "to disseminate accurate and timely information about topics of interest to on-site news media, and assist media personnel in obtaining access to information, individuals, and events that reinforce the strategic communications objectives of the United States and its allies".[13]

ARMY STRATEGIC COMMUNICATIONS

On August 1, 2003, General Peter J. Schoomaker became the thirty-fifth Chief of Staff of the Army. With a new chief came new ideas and concepts for how the Army would serve the Nation during the war on terrorism as well as integrating into the overall strategic vision of the Department of Defense. General Schoomaker established seventeen focus areas that would help guide the Army through the war on terrorism and transformation and would demonstrate the Army resolve to be a viable member of the Armed Forces.[14] One of the seventeen focus areas identified was the need for strategic communications. This would not be strategic communications in the form of a means for talking to forces deployed around the world, but instead communications that told the Army story, intertwined with the strategic communications efforts of the Office of the Secretary of Defense and the Joint Staff.

The Chief of Staff understood the importance of getting the message to the public, given the visibility of the Army in today's wartime environment. The intent of the Army's Strategic Communications Office was to ensure that the Army spoke with one voice across the force, with themes and messages that conveyed the Army's message from strategic down to tactical level. The program worked hand in hand with Army public affairs representatives to ensure total access for all media sources to provide the most relevant and accurate information available regarding all aspects of Army operations. It continually developed new themes and messages that addressed the critical issues and distributed them throughout the force and through all media outlets to ensure the widest dissemination of information. Each product that left the Army's Strategic Communications Office clearly reflected the Army Theme, as stated by the new Chief of Staff of the Army:

> Our Army is at war with nearly 50 percent of its forces engaged in combat. We will continue to be for the foreseeable future. Our Army is a proud member of the Joint Force expertly serving our Nation and its citizens as we continuously strive toward new goals and improve performance. Our Soldiers, their training, readiness, and welfare, are central to all we do. Our individual and organizational approach to our duties and tasks must reflect the seriousness of sense of urgency characteristic of an Army at War. Our Soldiers and our Nation deserve nothing less. We are at war.[15]

This focus on the Army at war and the professionalism of soldiers is simply one more means of bolstering the will of the American people as the Army continues to prosecute the War on Terror. In this war, as in most operations, the Air Force, Navy, and to some degree, the Marine Corps, only participated fully in the initial combat operations, leaving the preponderance of peacekeeping operations to the Army. It is critical that the Army understand the importance of using information operations to maintain support for their deployed forces, and the Chief of Staff of the Army is providing that focus to his leaders.

HISTORICAL USE OF THE MEDIA IN WAR PRIOR TO THE GLOBAL WAR ON TERRORISM

Before we examine Information Operations in the Global War on Terrorism more closely, we should review past wars and our use of information to execute national strategy. This review will allow us to use the lessons of history in our current war.

Prior to the Civil War, the United States had few reporters, and those who were in that business seldom had the means to cover the war, nor did they have a means to share the information from the war zone to the general population across the country. Therefore, the public interaction in war was limited only to those who received communications directly from soldiers.

Civil War

During the Civil War, censorship was the rule of the day, and reporters were subject to courts martial if they disclosed sensitive information; yet censorship was barely and unevenly applied. Journalism was both competitive and profitable, and editors devoted reporters specifically to covering the war. This coverage was so broad and uncontrolled that reporters frequently revealed troop movements and future plans. General Lee reportedly studied northern newspapers because they disclosed useful military information.[16] In this author's opinion, information operations in this war had little impact on national will because the United States was a country divided in the war.

World Wars I and II

When the United States entered World War I, the government imposed strict censorship on reporters. Those reporters in the war zone were required to be accredited, and they cooperated fully with the restrictions placed upon them.[17] Their patriotic coverage resulted in the full support of the American people for the war effort. As the United States entered World War II, both military and political leaders recognized the importance of press coverage of the war to maintain public support for the war.[18] The same procedure for censorship carried into World War II. Only those reporters who agreed to full military censorship were given accreditation and allowed into the war theater.[19] The Office of Censorship, with its 11,000 employees, made decisions to delete, delay, or suppress all or portions of any reports, despite the lack of any legal enforcement authority.[20] Most reporters accepted the censorship on their own and avoided reporting on forbidden topics, such as troop movements or upcoming operations. Philip Knightley, author of "The First Casualty: The War Correspondent as Hero, Propagandist, and Myth Maker," accused correspondents of only reporting what the government wanted told.[21] However, other World War II journalists disagree with this. Sir Theodore Bray, an editor during World War II with over fifty years in journalism, said in an interview, "The country was submitted to censorship in the interests of military and civilian morale. A lot of people now have forgotten that once a country goes to war, the country's got to change its attitude towards the media, and the media's got to change its attitude towards authority."[22]

Korean War

The Korean War began with voluntary censorship, but reports of early losses brought military complaints and resulted in the imposition of mandatory censorship within the first six months of the war.[23] Reporters not complying with the rules for censorship could lose their privileges or become subject to courts martial for their offenses.[24] By the end of the war, both the media and the military seemed to have agreed that military censorship was the solution to the inherent conflict in their goals.[25]

Vietnam War

The Vietnam War was a watershed event in media coverage of war. In the years after the Korean War, media outlets grew, communications technology enhanced the ability to gather news, and television matured into a real media force. This changed the government's perception of their ability to use censorship as the way to control information, and eventually, the military disbanded all of its censorship units.[26] Reporters found Vietnam fully accessible to them, and they accepted voluntary ground rules. Failure to adhere to the ground rules would mean the reporter could not move outside of Saigon, nor would he receive any cooperation. It was an effective control, and only nine incidences where these rules were violated were recorded throughout the duration of the war.[27] However, early, inaccurate reporting and information spins by the political leadership in order to gain public support for intervention in Vietnam created initial distrust between journalists and the military. The daily military briefings did not portray the same information that journalists had seen for themselves out in the field with units. Some reporters then focused on the negative in reporting. Most of their reports were true, but they focused on subjects unpopular with military leaders—a lack of discipline in units, the prevalent use of drugs by soldiers, and troops who questioned the United States' war aims. The final straw was misleading and negative reporting on the Tet offensive, which the military attributed to the unfavorable turn in public support for the war.[28]

Grenada

In the Grenada invasion in October 1983, the government banned the media for the first two days of the operation. On the third day, under a great deal of pressure, the military granted access only to a small pool of fifteen reporters out of the nearly seven hundred in Barbados.[29] This limitation was so unpopular with the media that, soon after the operation, the Secretary of Defense developed and released the Principles of Information, which stated:

> It is the policy of the Department of Defense to make available timely and accurate information so that the public, Congress, and members representing the press, radio, and television may assess and understand the facts about national security and defense strategy.[30]

Following the Grenada invasion, the Chairman of the Joint Chiefs of Staff, General John Vessey, appointed a commission to determine how the military should handle the media in future operations. In 1984, he appointed retired Army Major General Winant Sidle to head the panel, which included newsmen, public affairs officers, and operations officers.[31] The Statement of Principle from the Sidle Panel expanded upon the Department of Defense Principles of Information:

> The American people must be informed about the United States' military operations, and this information must be provided through both the news media and the government. Therefore, the panel believes it is essential that the U.S. news media cover U.S. military operations to the maximum degree possible consistent with mission security and the safety of U.S. forces.[32]

7

The panel also provided eight recommendations to improve operations. One of these was the establishment of ground rules for the press to follow in reporting military operations. Another of the eight recommendations from the Sidle Panel identified the need for press pools. In response, the Department of Defense established the National Media Pool (NMP), a standing pool of reporters carefully selected to provide widest dissemination of information in the early stages of an operation.[33]

Panama

The first test of the National Media Pool occurred in the Panama invasion in December 1989; the results were poor. Due to political concerns over the ability of the press pool to preserve operational security, reporters were notified and flown in late, missing the initial invasion.[34] This failure resulted in a renewed emphasis by the military on getting it right with the press. General Colin Powell, Chairman of the Joint Chiefs of Staff, issued guidance to military commanders reminding them of the importance of media aspects of military operations and of the need to plan media coverage and support requirements along with the operation.[35]

Desert Storm

The National Media Pool accompanied the first troops into Saudi Arabia in August 1990 and operated effectively for the first two weeks. However, as U.S. troops flowed into the theater, so did journalists. So many news outlets had reporters in the country (over 1600 at one point) that the NMP became ineffective, and the military began to see the challenges of a large number of reporters. Public Affairs Offices grouped journalists who wanted access to military units into small pools with escort officers, and the military units provided transportation. However, limitations on transportation with military units and the vast distances covered in the operation resulted in many journalists covering operations from hotels and reporting information from the formal briefings provided by the military. Many reporters were unsatisfied. While there was no censorship in place, the inability of journalists to move freely about during the combat operation resulted in managed reporting.[36]

8

Haiti

Operation Uphold Democracy was the first operation to plan for merging the media into units before operations began. The NMP was briefed on the plans for the invasion and reporters were given access to combat units prior to the operation. Although accords prevented the need for the invasion, the planning process validated the need for media involvement before operations began.[37]

The Balkans

In late December 1995, the Army decided to embed about two dozen reporters in the units deploying into Bosnia for Operation Joint Forge. Reporters become integral parts of their assigned units; the goal was full access to the operation for journalists and positive stories for the Army. In addition, this teaming would generate greater support from the American people and boost morale for soldiers. Despite some controversial stories publicized as a result of the close relationship of the journalist with the unit, the practice was deemed a success and continued throughout the deployment of units for stabilization force operations in Operation Joint Endeavor. In contrast, the Kosovo air campaign was marked by a gag order issued by NATO's Supreme Allied Commander, General Wesley Clark.[38] After the air campaign, journalists were allowed limited access into military units, but it was too late to change the perception of a lack of cooperation between the military and the media. This action set back the successes experienced during operations in Bosnia.

GLOBAL WAR ON TERRORISM

A review of the changes in the relationship of the military to the media throughout history shows that the most effective means of influencing national will is to establish a close relationship between reporters and soldiers. The most effective way to do this is to embed reporters in front line units.

In Operation Enduring Freedom, journalists once again flowed into theater along with soldiers in an effort to promote aggressive information operations. However, quite early on, reporters found themselves locked in a warehouse to prevent coverage of the return of soldiers killed and injured by a stray bomb. This action led to a written apology by Victoria Clarke, the Assistant Secretary of Defense for Public Affairs. Acknowledging the responsibility to provide correspondents the opportunity to cover the war, while balancing operational security and safety of the military, the Department of Defense renewed efforts to allow the media to provide information to the American people.[39] In January 2003, the Office of Global Communications was established and began its efforts to keep both the American public and the international community up-to-date on efforts in the war on terror. Planning for Operation Iraqi Freedom included an aggressive use of information operations. Strategic communications teams were allocated to the Central Command to ensure that the message on the success of the United States strategy in Iraq passed to the world.[40] Additionally, the Department of Defense, in a deliberate process, developed a program for ensuring complete media coverage of the operation. In February 2003, the Department of Defense published guidance and policies on embedding news media during possible future operations in the Central Command Region. The implementing message specifically identified that,

> [M]edia coverage of any future operation will, to a large extent, shape public perception of the national security environment now and in the years ahead. This holds true for the U.S. public; the public in allied countries whose opinion can affect the durability of our coalition; and publics in countries where we conduct operations, whose perceptions of us can affect the cost and duration of our involvement. Our ultimate strategic success in bringing peace and security to this region will come in our long-term commitment to supporting our democratic ideals.[41]

The message further directed that the means of achieving this objective would be through the use of embedded media with military units. These embeds would live, work, and travel with units, facilitating maximum coverage of combat and other operations.

Prior to the beginning of Operation Iraqi Freedom, the Office of the Assistant Secretary of Defense for Public Affairs vetted the journalists and allocated the embed opportunities to the various media organizations.[42] As a result, when operations began against Iraq in March 2003, over six hundred journalists were embedded in military units at all levels within the theater.[43] Within minutes of the execution of operations, media outlets were flooded with footage of U.S. and coalition troops in Iraq. Thanks to 24-hour news coverage, the public watched the steady advance to Baghdad and repeatedly saw the toppling of the symbols of the Iraqi regime, most notably the statues of Saddam Hussein. Because of the embed process, the public also saw many details of the life of the American military and came to appreciate the sacrifices these individuals make to execute the Nation's security strategy. Every day in their living rooms, Americans saw the actions of real heroes, because the embedded journalist was there to report the heroic actions immediately. Never before had the military been so successful in portraying their operations to the American public. The result was an outpouring of support and overwhelming pride in the American military force.

As the President announced the end of major combat operations, the embedded journalists left the units they had become a part of and returned to their normal operations. Some stayed in Iraq to cover other aspects of the Iraqi story, while many returned to their news agencies and other stories. By the summer of 2003, only a fraction of the original number of journalists remained in the country. Additionally, the strategic communications teams withdrew from the Central Command Headquarters, leaving a void in the coverage of the continuing Operation Iraqi Freedom. With the end of major combat operations came other changes in U.S. security strategy. As the national focus changed to diplomatic efforts to establish a new government for the people of Iraq, the military operation became a struggling balance of fighting insurgents while trying to stabilize the country.

ASSESSMENT

During combat operations in Iraq, information operations were successfully used to promote U.S. successes in fighting the Iraqi regime. Strategic communications teams at the combatant command level facilitated the broadcast of the U.S. government's themes and messages throughout the world. Embedded journalists told the military story, first hand and in real time, in a way the world had never seen before. Additionally, they served to meet the needs of the global communications office by being on hand at the flash points around the world where U.S. interests were in the spotlight. The military made tremendous strides in its relationship with the media, and that is the greatest success story of all.

Although there were extremely few limitations placed on the embedded journalists, either through policy or practice, there are those who criticize this success. Some journalists and scholars took issue with how the embeds actually performed and felt that the U.S. Government used them as a propaganda stunt, providing only the images the U.S. leadership wanted the world to view.[44]

With the disbanding of the embedded media in units and the disestablishment of the strategic communications team at Central Command headquarters, the success of information operations was reduced. The continuing violence and instability in Iraq warranted continued strategic communications support, as did both U.S. military and international agency efforts to rebuild the country. Without the embedded media representatives in units, reporters who saw the entire spectrum of operations and knew the people involved, the media coverage tended to focus on the negative aspects of operations in Iraq. Seldom did they report the good news stories of medical support to the Iraqi people, children returning to school, and Iraqis taking charge of their lives. Because of the negative focus, the American public and the international community only saw very short sound bites by the various media representatives from the same spot at the Palestine Hotel, usually reporting American casualties. There was no collaborative effort between the government and the media to tie these casualties to efforts underway throughout the country. In September 2003, Torie Clarke, the former Assistant Secretary of Defense for Public Affairs and Pentagon spokesperson, acknowledged that the significant change in coverage caused new problems for the administration. "We went from hundreds of journalists all over Iraq covering every aspect of the War, I don't know what the number is now but it's a fraction of that now and I think that is too bad. There are some important things going on in that country. Many are good, some are bad, but if there was coverage and more comprehensive coverage people would get a clearer picture."[45]

Without the emphasis of the strategic communications team focusing the themes or messages, working hand in hand with the media to convey the actual strategic goals, an even larger void developed within the Middle East region. Some challenge the overall National Security Strategy for the Middle East and divert the focus from the war on terrorism to issues about morals, values, religious practices, or even the desire for oil.[46] In the absence of U.S. media and daily briefings arranged for all the available journalists, international journalists have the tendency to slant the news in accordance with their national or, in some cases, religious beliefs. "The Middle East media and regimes' uncontested blaming of western culture over many years for their unjust conditions causes the common person in the Middle East to develop mistrust and ill feelings toward the western culture and perpetuates the ill feelings towards the infidels."[47] Some leaders in the Middle East are taking advantage of the unchecked propaganda about U.S. involvement in the region to promote their own interests. Strategic communications is one of the most effective means of perpetuating our National Security Strategy throughout the world, yet we failed to recognize the need to continue those efforts after combat operations. "The National Security Strategy's inadequacy to build favorable public relations in the Middle East directly contributed to the strong Arab public anger that has been directed at the US. However, a greater strategic loss resulted from Arab officials that privately supported the United States, but publicly supported and sponsored demonstrations against the U.S. government's plans in Iraq."[48]

The war on terrorism continues and so must the efforts of the Office of Global Communications. Without question, the organization achieved its intent through the military instrument of power for the initial phase of war with Iraq and the overall war on terrorism. However, it also must recognize some failures. Once major combat operations ended in Iraq, there seemed to be a lack of coordiNation amongst the various agencies to promote a standard, recurring message that took full advantage of all elements of national power. Additionally, the policy executors continued to miss the mark by not getting the full utilization of the media to publicize the desired themes and messages versus the selected agenda of junior reporters.

Both the administration and the military recognized the downhill spiral the communications strategy took and apparently realized they must get the program back on track. Cognizant of the impact the media plays on the National Security Strategy, and desiring the media's output to serve as a strategic enabler, efforts appear underway to effectively communicate the objectives and desired end state for Iraq to the international community and the American public. The military has once again become proactive in using the media to cover all aspects of the operations ongoing in Iraq and other regions where United States or coalition forces are fighting the war on terrorism. Emphasis is now on daily press briefings by the senior military leadership in the Iraqi theater to provide up-to-date status on both positive and negative activities within the area of responsibility.

Additionally, the Department of Defense has gone on the offense in dealing with the media's "armchair generals," to make them completely aware of activities within the region. Many of the guest commentators lack actual first-hand information and express their views based on prior experiences and on the raw data received from field journalists. To facilitate a more accurate assessment by this specific body of reporters, the Pentagon has arranged trips to the Middle East for the experts to get first-hand accounts and a personal assessment of the overall situation.[49]

In an effort to engage the other aspects of national power, specifically the diplomatic and economic elements, the administration has begun to engage in more routine appearances with the media. Obviously, much effort has gone into synchronizing the message the various senior representatives send to the American public and to the international community as a whole. The senior United States diplomat in Iraq, Paul Bremer, increased his efforts to push the U.S. strategy for the country as well. He has aggressively addressed the U.S. goals for Iraq in numerous print articles and broadcast interviews. Both scheduled and unscheduled press briefings serve to perpetuate the message. This media blitz, coupled with the increased presence of senior administration officials, specifically the Secretary of State, Secretary of Defense, and even the Vice President of the United States, on the news talk show circuit, hammers away at the same strategic goals for Iraq. From this, we can see the increased emphasis in the media on the government's agenda rather than the media's. This technique, properly orchestrated by the Office for Global Communications, will have far-reaching impact for the administration with both allies and terrorist organizations. One of the most powerful attributes of the media is their ability to touch all people through either print or television. However, the administration must be careful to be accurate and honest with their messages, because the media judges them daily and has the potential of causing more turmoil than good, if the government is not honest or sends mixed messages.[50]

RECOMMENDATIONS

The establishment of the Office of Global Communications was an important step in using information to build both national and international support for U.S. initiatives around the world. However, some changes must occur in order for this office to be totally successful.

The global communications policy must assist in the accomplishment of the National Security Strategy by applying equally to all the instruments of power, not just the military element. Additional emphasis should go toward the establishment of the strategic communications teams to support military and civilian leaders that are on the forward edge of the battlefield, fighting the war on terrorism, and promoting the United States government's goals and interests. The following proposals will provide this emphasis:

- the Office of Global Communications should establish permanent strategic communications teams in all the combatant commands to provide a realistic, daily focus on operations around the world.

- the administration must use the Office of Global Communications to develop themes and messages for all aspects of future operations—military, economic, and diplomatic—prior to initiating the operation.

- immediately place a strategic communications team with Ambassador Bremer's organization to publicize the daily successes in Iraq throughout the world.

The media is a valuable resource that leaders at all levels need to utilize to convey the message of the day. With the Nation engaged around the globe in fighting the war on terrorism, the use of media resources is essential to reaching the world populace and explaining the United States' position and strategy for ridding the world of terrorists. Through proper use of the Office of Global Communications, the United States can truly influence and strengthen the will of the American people and our alliances to defeat global terrorism.

ENDNOTES

1. George W. Bush, *The National Security Strategy of the United States of America* (Washington, D.C.: The White House, September 27, 2003), pg 1.

2. Ibid., 1.

3. Ibid., 1.

4. Ibid., 5.

5. Ibid., 6.

6. Ibid. , 1.

7. Ibid. , 6.

8. Presidential Documents, Executive Order 13283 of January, 21, 2003, *Federal Register,* Vol. 68, No.16, sec. 1, January 24, 2003.

9. Ibid., sec. 2.

10. Ibid., sec. 3.

11. Ibid.

12. Ibid.

13. Ibid.

14. Handout to U.S. Army War College Current Affairs Panel, Chief of Staff of the Army Focus Areas, received 16 November 2003.

15. U.S. Army Theme, Relevant and Ready. available from <http:://www. army.mil/ features/relevant andready/index.html>; Internet; accessed 10 December 2003.

16. Thomas W. Hall II, "The Military and the Media: Toward a Strategy of Engagement and Enlargement," April 1995.

17. Ibid.

18. Ibid.

19. Barry E. Venable, "The Army and the Media," *Military Review,* January–February 2002, available from <http://www-cgsc.army.mil/milrev/ English/JanFeb02/venable.asp>; Internet; accessed 30 December 2003.

20. Hall.

21. ABC Radio National – Media Report Transcript, "Censorship During the Second World War," August 17, 1995, available from <http://www.avc.net. au/rn/talks/8.30/mediarpt/mstories/ mr170801.htm>; Internet; accessed 30 December 2003.

22. Ibid.

23. Hall.

24. Venable.

25. Major General Winant Sidle, "The Gulf War Reheats Military-Media Controversy," *Military Review,* September 1991, available from <https://calldbp.leavenworth.army.mil/scripts/ cqcgi.exe/@ss_prod. env?CQ_ SESSION_KE...>; Internet; accessed 30 December 2003.

26. Ibid.

27. Ibid.

28. Ibid.

29. Ibid.

30. Venable.

31. Ibid.

32. Ibid.

33. Ibid.

34. Ibid.

35. Ibid.

36. Sidle.

37. Venable.

38. Margaret H. Belknap, The CNN Effect: Strategic Enabler or Operational Risk? *Parameters US Army War College Quarterly,* Autumn 2002, available from <http://www.carlisle. army.mil/usawc/parameters/02autumn/ belknap.htm>; Internet; accessed 23 September 2003.

39. Stephen Lee, "Media Access in War," January 28,2003, available from <http://www. newsaic.com/ftvsnl 27-06p.html>; Internet; accessed 2 January 2004.

40. BG Vincent Brooks, comments during the embedded media workshop at Carlisle Barracks, 3-5 September 2003.

41. Secretary of Defense Message, Public Affairs Guidance (PAG) on Embedding Media During Possible Future Operations/Deployments in the U.S. Central Commands (CENTCOM) Area of Responsibility, 101900zFeb03.

42. Ibid.

43. Peter Johnson, "Clarke Aims for Clearer View," *USA Today,* 25 September 2003, pg 6; available from <https://www.us.army.mil/portal/jhtml/ earlyBird/Sep003/e2003092521964.html>; Internet; accessed 25 September 2003.

44. Jennie Bristow.

45. Peter Johnson.

46. George (Sam) Hamontree, U.S. National Security Strategy in The Middle East Operational Victories and Strategic Setbacks, Defence Systems Daily, 22 August 2003, available from <http://defence-data.com/features/fpage51.htm>; Internet; accessed 23 September 2003.

47. Ibid.

48. Ibid.

49. Elaine M. Grossman, Pentagon Takes Television Defense Pundits on Tour of Occupied Iraq, Inside the Pentagon, September 25, 2003, pg1, available from <https://www.us.army.mil/ portal/jhtml/earlyBird/Sep2003?e20030925219449.html>; Internet; accessed 25 September 2003.

50. Gervase Pearce, Arm Chair Strategy, October 2001, pg4, available from <http://www. spiraldynamics.com/ documents/hotspots/Afghanistan/pearce armchair.htm>; Internet; accessed 27 September 2003.

BIBLIOGRAPHY

ABC Radio National – Media Report Transcript, "Censorship During the Second World War."Available from <http://wwwabc.net.au/rn/talks/8.30/ mediarpt/mstories/mr170801.htm>. Internet. Accessed 30 December 2003.

Belknap, Margaret H. "The CNN Effect: Strategic Enabler or Operational Risk?" *Parameters US Army War College Quarterly*, Autumn 2002. Available from <http:www.carlisle.army.mil/usawc/ parameters/02autumn/belknap. htm>. Internet. Accessed 23 September 2003.

Bristow, Jennie. "Strange Embedded Fellows." *Spiked Politics*, Article 27, March 2003. Available from <http://www.spiked-online.com/Printable/ 00000006DD17.htm>. Internet.Accessed 23 September 2003.

Brooks, Vincent, comments during the embedded media workshop at Carlisle Barracks, 3-5 September 2003.

Bush, George W. The National Security Strategy of the United States Of America. Washington, D.C. : The White House, 27 September 2003.

Grossman, Elaine M. "Pentagon Takes Television Defense Pundits on Tour of Occupied Iraq" *Inside the Pentagon* 25 September 2003, pg1. Available from <http://www.carlisle.army.mil/portal/jhtml/earlyBird/ Sep2003?e20030925219449.html>. Internet. Accessed 25 September 2003.

Hall, Thomas W. *The Military and the Media: Toward a Strategy of Engagement and Enlargement.* Maxwell Air Force Base, Alabama: Air University, April 1995.

Hamontree, George. "U.S. National Security Strategy in the Middle East Operational Victories and Strategic Setbacks" *Defence Systems Daily* 22 August 2003. Available from http://defence-data.com/features/fpage51. htm>. Internet. Accessed 23 September 2003.

Handout to U.S. Army War College Current Affairs Panel, Chief of Staff of the Army Focus Areas, received 16 November 2003.

Johnson, Peter. "Clarke Aims for Clearer View" *USA Today* 25 September 2003, pg6. Available from<https://www.us.army.mil/portal/jhtml/earlyBird/ Sep2003/e20030925219644.html>. Internet. Accessed 25 September 2003.

Lee, Stephen. "Media Access in War," January 28, 2002. Available from <http://www.newsaic.com/ftvsn/27-06p.html>. Internet. Accessed 2 January 2004.

Pearce, Gervase. "Arm Chair Strategy" October 2001, pg4. Available from <http://www.spiraldynamics.com/documents/hotspots/Afghanistan/pearce.armchair.htm>. Internet. Accessed 27 September 2003.

Presidential Documents, Executive Order 13283 of January 21, 2003, *Federal Register,* Vol.68, No.16, sec. 1, 24 January 2003.

Secretary of Defense Message, "Public Affairs Guidance (PAG) on Embedding Media During Possible Future Operations/Deployments in the U.S. Central Commands (CENTCOM) Area of Responsibility (AOR), 101900zFeb03.

Sidle, Major General Winant. "The Gulf War Reheats Military – Media Controversy," *Military Review*, Command and General Staff College, September 1991. Available from <https://calldbp.leavenworth.army.mil/scripts/cqcgi.ee/@ss_prod.env?CQ_SESSION_ KE...>. Internet. Accessed 30 December 2003.

Venable, Barry E. "The Army and the Media" *Military Review*, Command and General Staff College, January – February 2002. Available from <http://www-cgsc.army.mil/milrev/ english/JanFeb02/venable.asp>. Internet. Accessed 30 December 2003.

CHAPTER 2

THE MEDIA AND NATIONAL SECURITY DECISION MAKING

Lieutenant Colonel James M. Marye
United States Army

The media's role in influencing national and international public opinion through around-the-clock coverage of worldwide events has grown immensely in today's ever more connected world. This phenomenon has led media makers of both television and the Internet to an even greater role in influencing high-level, national-level decision making. The media, with modern communication technology and direct access to the front lines, has made decision makers, and the public they serve, acutely aware of situations presented in "raw" form in almost real time, with little or no substantiation or corroboration against which opinions and decisions are rendered. This research paper will demonstrate that, more than any other time in history, the media, by embedding reporters within military units, has affected public opinion and moved decisions made at the national level. This does not imply that decisions made are solely with the media in mind, but that the media, especially if they are embedded, are a potent criterion that must be considered when developing a strategy and maintaining its theme. This paper will also recommend enhancements to the present embedded media program that may help give the public and national decision makers higher quality information.

In past decades, the public and their decision makers relied on print media, then print media and news reels followed by television—which underwent its own evolution—paralleled by the evolution of computers and the creation of the internet, leading to communications innovations that have revolutionized media reporting capabilities. This evolutionary process has changed news coverage forever. The constant bombardment of reports from the embedded reporters on the frontlines in Iraq made the general public feel as if they were part of the war, and they wanted immediate answers from their political and military leaders. This presented a new and complicated challenge to the country's leadership, who at all levels were desperately trying to answer the multitude of questions being asked of them. The embedded process has helped sell the military as a viable institution performing its duty for the Nation , but it has also complicated the decision maker's world and grown the power of the media within the informational element of national power.

INFORMATION ELEMENT OF POWER

The media plays an important role in high-level decision making and strategy formulation. It is not necessarily the adversary of the military that many think, but can be a very valuable asset, as demonstrated in the embedded program. Possibly thought of as a muscular component within the informational element of power, the media can provide another weapon in an arsenal used to attack the enemy psychologically as well as to gain public support within one's own nation. The media can affect the morale of enemy soldiers and that of the citizens of their nations, whose support will wane if unhappy with the political-military situation. The same is true for the United States. Without the support of the public, the cause is soon forgotten and the morale of the military is adversely affected, as we have seen in past conflicts. In the recent Iraqi conflict, the embedded media program tied the American public to the soldiers fighting for the Nation . The media is a valuable tool to the strategists, but they must remember that honesty between the military and the media is imperative, for once the military's integrity is compromised, this informational tool can become their greatest nemesis.

The media is a strong instrument of national power due to its incredible influence over our adversary as well as our own public. Near "real-time" news coverage has altered the decision-making process and influences our ability, as well as that of our adversary, to quickly manage its effects. This also works in reverse and, used properly, will affect the decision-making cycle of an adversary targeted in an informational operations campaign. In the past, much of the "third world" was in an information void with no access to global events, but this has changed, largely due to the expansion and availability of multimedia reception as well as communications devices. During Operation Enduring Freedom (OEF) as well as Operation Iraqi Freedom (OIF), it was common to see Bedouin nomads in the most austere portion of the desert talking on a satellite telephone. Now, one may argue that they were more than just

22

Bedouin herders, but the real shock is that someone in the middle of nowhere, riding a camel, has the ability to communicate anywhere in the world. This is not just advancement in technology, but the evolution and dispersion of informational power.

Technological advances in communication throughout the United States alone provide immediate feedback to national decision makers. Reactionary style decision making, due to the immediacy of information, will force the strategist to use the media as criteria during the planning process. Understanding the media and the singular power it possesses can allow the strategist to make much more informed decisions by treating the media as a critical element of power. The strategist must take the bad with the good and understand that this relationship and its impact on national security decision making is extremely complex and requires a great degree of care and cultural change. This change within the military is underway, as evidenced through the acceptance of the embedded media, but those last few leaders who refuse to embrace it and never fully understand its power are fated to receive its potential wrath. In terms of "**ends, ways,** and **means**," the media is a **means** by which to alter and influence enemy actions so as to reach the strategist's desired **ends.**

From Vietnam To Iraq

"Was the United States defeated in the jungles of Vietnam, or was it defeated in the streets of American cities?" Colonel Paul Vallely and Major Michael Aquino asked, in a 1980 article for *Military Review* in which they posited that the United States had "lost the war—not because we were outfought, but because we were out PSYOPed." They felt that the media had failed to "defend the U.S. public against the propaganda of the enemy." This ability to influence public opinion through the media and to influence the media itself are much the same tactics that current day terrorists use to gain support for their cause and to negatively influence the public's support of their adversary. This is not to say that operational and tactical commanders make poor decisions, but the time to analyze, develop, and arrive at a decision is acutely abbreviated. Many factors influence this, and the increasing public awareness on global issues, thanks to the abundance of information, makes this a complex task. The attention and support Americans give to an issue is in direct proportion to the amount of press coverage it receives. [1] The media is a

23

moneymaking business and focuses on stories that sell, which are largely centered on sensational events. Images of the suffering, dead, and mass destruction not only sway public opinion, but can distort policymakers' perceptions of the crisis as well.[2] There is no longer a filter between the public and the event. The events presented by the media in Vietnam were perceived to be true to much of the American public and to many of the Nation 's decision makers. Press coverage, specifically television, changed the perception of warfare, beginning with the Vietnam War. The public was able to see the grotesque images of war up front, no longer separated by thousands of miles. These horrible images, which were previously only heard or read about, now faced them head on. Our soldiers were dying daily as it became an "in your face" war. There was no hiding from these images broadcast globally, and the government was forced to deal with this new effect on public opinion.

In October of 1983, the United States, with the support of neighboring Caribbean states, invaded Grenada to oust the People's Revolutionary Government and protect U.S. citizens in an effort to restore the state's legitimate government.[3] With the memories of Vietnam still fresh in the minds of the U.S. leadership, the press was not allowed to participate in the invasion. There was great concern over the operational security of the mission and the possibility of the press endangering its success as well as the lives of the military involved. Additionally, there was possibly the concern over broadcasting problems the United States may encounter and was not prepared to handle, or did so poorly. The plan had excluded the media completely from the operation until the leadership was convinced they could do no harm.[4] "There were no firsthand reports from Grenada until two and a half days after the operation began. The media, citing the American people's right to know and frustrated at their inability to provide the level of reporting that they would have liked, protested loudly about the military's gross oversight in failing to permit journalists to accompany the operation."[5] The media would have obviously picked up on the communication problems that the invading force encountered as well as the lack in topographical information available for Grenada.[6] Due to poor interaction between the media and the military, a panel was formed to determine the best way to conduct military operations while keeping the public informed.[7] The answer the panel came up with was the Department of Defense National Media Pool (DoDNMP) or the "press pool."

In December 1989, in response to General Noriega's declaration of war, the United States invaded Panama, principally in support of treaty obligations to ensure the unhindered operation of the Panama Canal, and to protect the lives of U.S. citizens and their property as well as restore a legitimate democracy to the isthmus. This time, the press was pulled into the operation based on decisions that came about as a result of the Grenada invasion; however, they were still disgruntled, since the "press pool" didn't provide the access that they had envisioned.

U.S. Southern Command had made no plans for the press to accompany any of the units; thus, none of the media witnessed any actual combat. In fact, the independent journalists were "sequestered" and detained at Howard Air Force Base, presumably for their safety.[8] Additionally, the media was ill prepared to cover the war. They had experienced numerous problems in their initial planning, which translated into poor logistical support as well as limited capability to file a story once in country.[9] Media involvement in military operations still had a long way to go, and although not the complete lockout as in Grenada, the "press pool" concept was not providing adequate access to the action, and media logistical support needed greater emphasis in its planning.

Saddam Hussein's invasion of Kuwait resulted in the buildup of U.S. forces in 1990 and the kickoff of the First Gulf War in January 1991. The United States led a coalition that ousted the Iraqi force from Kuwait and penetrated deep into Iraq for a resounding defeat of Saddam's forces. The operation was a great success, yet the press still experienced problems in regard to access to the troops and action. They were forced to always be accompanied by a Public Affairs Officer anytime they spoke with the troops and to have their stories reviewed by the military and passed back through military communicative means. Even when their stories did reach the United States, they claimed censorship due to the delay experienced by this process. Although included into the plan this time, U.S. Central Command dictated their every movement on the battlefield and reviewed each report prior to release. This was far from the unfettered access the press had envisioned.[10]

President George H.W. Bush ordered U.S. troops into action in December of 1992 to restore order in Somalia, which at that time was in the middle of a civil war and mass starvation. This presented new challenges for both the press and the military. The battle of Mogadishu turned out to be the most intensive close combat that Americans had faced since the Vietnam War.[11] The unfettered access the press had to the battlefield during this operation was dramatic. This was the very thing that the military and national leadership had feared in the previously mentioned vignettes.

The media most assuredly shaped public opinion and ultimately became the catalyst for the U.S. pullout. As mentioned earlier, images of starving children and of dead U.S. servicemen being dragged through the streets of Mogadishu were shocking. "The media's access to the battlefield influenced operations in a manner previously unseen. Consider the frustration that the U.S. troops felt when the international press corps reported on the Task Force Rangers' seemingly bungled raid on a U.S. compound in Mogadishu in August 1993. Three days later, a U.S. Army Quick Reaction Force patrol approached a suspected military mortar firing position that was housed in a humanitarian relief organization compound, and this time they knocked on the gate and asked permission to search." The media had influenced the actions of the patrol.[12]

Today, the presence of CNN and other news agencies on the battlefield may influence the combat leader's decisiveness and the decisions made by both his military and political superiors. The public, through the eye of the media, will see a situation unfold at the same time as the military leadership, making media involvement an important criterion to be used in crisis analyses in order to produce a viable course of action. Access to real-time global events has added a new and critical step in the decision-making process. Public opinion changes rapidly and is influenced heavily by visual images seen on television. Additionally, mobile communications, facsimiles, and the Internet have made access to both political and military decision makers more available than in the past. Further enhancing this effect today is the proliferation of the personal computer. The public has access to immediate information on about any topic or event. Computer speed has doubled every twelve to eighteen months for several years. This means that raw information is sent so quickly that there is no time to prepare or react, and in most cases the public sees it as it occurs. This "real-time" flow of information can and often will adversely impact the reaction time a leader has to make a decision and limit the ability to analyze its affects. Time is the most critical resource in analyzing a problem, and now it has become even more so with the ability to see a crisis event as it is unfolding. Due to this global awakening, a single person can have strategic impact on world events. This may also influence the ability to make rapid decisions in a very constrained timeline.

The Media And Recent National Security Decision Making

Did the "Yellow Press drive President George W. Bush to war" or did he use the press to open the door?[13] The war in Iraq certainly had many different strategic and political motivators. There is no doubt of Saddam Hussein's cruelty to his own people and his ability to obtain and manufacture weapons of mass destruction (WMD). His use of chemical agents on his own people is proof of his willingness to use WMD on an adversary. Was this reasoning enough to make a unilateral decision to go it alone and depose this "evil" dictator? The media most certainly played an incredibly large role in getting this message out. This information was easily used to help incite U.S. public opinion and support the President's position to go to war against Iraq. The U.S. Congress, also influenced by this information, saw themselves scrutinized as they deliberated this resolution to go to war in front of millions of viewers who were also their constituents.

This message presented by the media justified the President's decision to go to war. Some may argue that the decision was made well in advance; however, the media was used successfully to capture the deliberation within Congress. The American public continued to hear of this evil they would soon have to confront in order to make the world a safer place, and now they were able to see their elected representative either vote yes or no on this very important resolution. The pressure was on, and if one disagreed with the notion that war (a.k.a.—regime change) was the only alternative, the whole country would see it. This same tactic was also used in the attempt to secure United Nations (UN) approval. This time it was not as successful. However, the refusal of several security council member states was strongly admonished by the Bush administration and the world was able to see, even if an illusion, how this administration petitioned the UN unsuccessfully for help.

The media and the use of the media play a critical role in national security decision making. It can either be used to the advantage of the strategist or become a millstone. If the media is viewed as an asset and its use is truly understood, then it will only enable the strategist; however, if misunderstood and used incorrectly, it will most certainly force the strategist to react prematurely and possibly without the support of public opinion. A new level of war is upon us where we receive an "endless" stream of information that can overwhelm us. This information will come from various sources and mostly from the media.[14] Not only will our decision-making process be hazy, but so too will our adversary's. The enemy will also have the burden to share of sorting out and interpreting all this information before he can make a decision and react.[15] This should be somewhat gratifying and comforting to know that the "bad guys" will also have a difficult time as well as be greatly influenced by the multitude of information media and the vast amount they must sift through in order to successfully use it.

EMBEDDED MEDIA

The decision to embed reporters during Operation Iraqi Freedom (OIF) was a skillfully devised strategic initiative executed flawlessly. Media influence works both ways on public opinion. The false idea that the press only wants to report the negative had forced some military leaders into a form of military isolation. No doubt, sensationalism sells, and the media is a business where good-news stories are generally not top sellers, but the "embedded reporter" was able to report on the good and bad at the grassroots level. The initial idea to embed reporters was met with not only skepticism from within the ranks of the military, but also among seasoned reporters who felt that embeds might lose their objectivity. Serving as part of the team and suffering the many uncomfortable situations the soldiers faced, which included daily life and death decisions, forced a bonding between reporter and soldier. The embedded reporter was less likely to focus on the bad and to have a real desire for a positive outcome. Another aspect of this plan was that by devoting a significant number of reporters at the front-line level, the press would have little time to invest in finding larger more controversial issues. The military portrayed to hometowns across America, through the media, their soldiers' sacrifices as they fought for our national objectives. This was possibly manipulation of the press; regardless, the situation benefited both the military and the media, and both were able to get an equitable return. The media is an inestimable tool in national and military decision making.

Many argue that public support is directly in proportion to the amount of media coverage given to a specific topic.[16] "Few humanitarian crises seem to produce a public response unless they have first attracted the attention of the press and television—the so called CNN-effect." General Anthony Zinni said that television has captured the initiative in defining the context in which events take place, how they are proceeding, and how the military, for example, is performing.[17] "We have to tune to CNN to see how we're doing." The power of the press is real and can shape national and international opinion; however, the power of the press can also be a positive influence in how we shape opinion in our favor. As much as the military has complained with regard to the negativism of the press, it has also successfully used the press in its information warfare campaign. The military has invested a lot of training and resources in its public affairs community. "Our message or theme" is well thought out and made available for public consumption, and the press is our messenger. As stated earlier, the press represents the truth and serves as the public's "whistle blower." When Americans distrust what comes out of the mouths of our national leaders, they still believe the media. National decision makers are learning that the press is a respected institution among Americans that can be an asset in their prosecution of the national agenda.

During Operation Enduring Freedom in Afghanistan, selected reporters were allowed access to the mission briefings and plans for Operation Anaconda. These same reporters accompanied the troops during the conduct of the operation. They were not allowed to report on any details or aspects of the mission until after the operation began and they had returned to the Forward Operations Base (FOB). The media not involved in the operation based their reports on speculation, which even though not totally factual could have jeopardized the operation. Not until their return from the operation did reporters like CNN's Martin Savage, and Sean Naylor for the Army Times get factual stories out. This caused a bit of angst initially, but it helped make the operation a success while simultaneously protecting the operation itself, those that fought in it, and those that reported on it. Margaret Belknap, in her article, *The*

CNN Effect: Strategic Enabler or Operational Risk, states that "the military attracts people who follow the rules; the media attract those who thrive on less is more," implying that the media will do whatever it takes to get a story as opposed to military personnel who will follow the rules given by their commanding officer.[18] The media involved in Operation Anaconda during OEF did a good job by protecting information and not releasing it until it was no longer a threat to those on the ground. Whether one subscribes to Margaret Belknap's theory or not, it is possible that, at times, what the media reports may not have all the details but may still impact the mission. This is possibly a good argument for the embedding of reporters who share the same risk as the soldier.

In the last century, the process of reporting on what occurred during a battle took several days to reach home, but due to technological advances, the time now is reduced to only hours or minutes. The luxury of time to react and craft the appropriate political statement is no more. It has become an immediate-action drill where a prepared sound bite is used in order to buy additional time. What a soldier does on the battlefield immediately affects national, as well as international, sentiment for or against a strategic cause. He is not just a soldier, one of many, but he is a "strategic soldier," capable of changing the entire image of a mission with a bad decision or a bullet that strays from its intended target.[19] "Big decisions are often made by military and political leaders, but the strategic soldier—by his one mistake that is sure to be televised—also affects the military operation." Embedded reporters were able to bring the individual soldier and unit actions directly to the American public and their national decision makers.

RECOMMENDATIONS

The military has made great progress with media relations, and the embedded program is the center of this recent success. To build on what has been accomplished, it is recommended that the following initiatives be reviewed for implementation.

1. There needs to be greater focus on media operations during training cycles at the Combat Training Centers.

2. Unit commanders and key unit officers must understand all facets of military-media relations. They must also fully comprehend the fact that there may be "bad" stories

reported at times. They must learn to take the good with the bad and to capitalize on what they learn from their mistakes.

3. Media training is essential at the lowest levels. It should be incorporated at all levels of Noncommissioned Officer Education System as well as officer professional development, starting with the Officer Basic Course. A good professional relationship between the military and the media is essential for success in future operations.

4. Embedded reporters from local media outlets should have first priority for assignment with military units from their state or local region so that they can both train and conduct operations with units familiar to them and their media audience.

5. Embedded reporters should be assigned to all levels of military command and throughout the interagency community.

6. Embedded reporters assigned to specific military headquarters must receive lessons in military planning and strategy in addition to mandatory media boot camp instruction.

7. Media training must become a mandatory requirement for staff level training and senior service college programs.

CONCLUSION

In a world of immediate access to information, our society wants constant updates on what is happening across our borders, especially in a time of war.[20] "CNN has the technology, the skills, and the money to go live anywhere in the world and can report 24/7 on a global stage before the live camera that never blinks.....Anytime there is military action taking place there will always be a CNN team member available in that specific area to report the action to the people."[21]

CNN, along with other news agencies, has shown the ability to travel to the unreachable place and report from an austere and hostile environment in "real time." This may influence the military's ability to make well-thought-out decisions, ranging from the strategic to the tactical level—distinctly separate levels that at times have become almost synonymous, thanks to the press. Strong images broadcast from around the world make a significant impact on public opinion. The sight of dead soldiers being dragged through the streets in Somalia was enough to enrage the public and influence the Clinton administration to abandon its efforts. Pictures of a war-torn country and starving children led the United States to finally introduce a military element into Liberia, where little or no U.S. national interests lie.[22] "The media by itself may not be enough to alter government policy, but a public becoming ever increasingly aware has the ability to make its voice heard in reaction to a media event." This can now be done through email, facsimile, and cellular communications all the way to Washington—from the constituency to the executive branch—almost instantaneously. [23]

The media's effect on national security decision making is significant. There is no doubt of its influence, and based on the information provided within this record, there can be no doubt of its power and effect on national security decision making. It has emerged as a viable element of power. Acceptance of this concept will allow the strategist to use information, the second element of power, to its fullest extent.

ENDNOTES

1. Burns, Alex, "Weapons of Mass Protection" War Reportage and Information Society, 11 March 2003, available from <http://www.disinfo.com/archive/pages/article/id1298/pg1/>, accessed 20 November 2003.

2. Fred Cate, "CNN effect, is not clear cut," *Humanitarian Affairs Review*, Summer 2002,available from <http://www.globalpolicy.org/ngos/aid/2002/summercnn.htm>, accessed 13 October 2003.

3. Bruner, Gary P., "Military-Media Relations in Recent U.S. Operations," 14 November 1997, available from< http://www.amsc.belvoir.army.mil/military.htm>, accessed 10 February 2004, p.2.

4. Ibid., 2.

5. Ibid., 2.

6. "Operation Urgent Fury," FAS Military Analysis Network, 27 May 1999, available from <http://www.fas.org/man/dod-101/ops/urgent_fury.htm>, assessed 10 February 2004, p.1.

7 Bruner, Gary P., "Military-Media Relations in Recent U.S. Operations," 14 November 1997, available from <http://www.amsc.belvoir.army.mil/military.htm>, accessed 10 February 2004, p.2.

8. Ibid., 3.

9. Ibid., 3.

10. Ibid. 3.

11. "Battle of Mogadishu," *Wikipedia The Free Encyclopedia*, available from <http://en.wikipedia.org/wiki/October_3_1993_Battle_of_Mogadishu>, accessed 10 February 2004.

12. Stockwell, David B., Major, "Press Coverage in Somalia," available from <http://www.globalsecurity.org/military/library/report/1995/SDB.htm>, accessed 10 February 2004.

13. Douglas V. Johnson II, "The Impact of the Media on National Security Policy Decision Making," (Carlisle: Strategic Studies Institute, 1994), 3.

14. Lafferty, Haywood, Klincar, Monteith, Strednansky, "The Impact of Media Information on Enemy Effectiveness: A Model for Conflict," *Proteus, A Journal of Ideas*, Spring 1994, p.30.

15. Ibid., 30.

16. Fred Cate, "CNN effect, is not clear cut," Humanitarian Affairs Review, Summer 2002,available from <http://www.globalpolicy.org/ngos/aid/2002/summercnn.htm>; accessed 13 October 2003.

17. "The Mass Media's Impact on International Affairs," U.S. Institute of Peace Watch, June 1997, available from <http://www.usip.org/peacewatch/1997/697/media.html>, accessed 17 November 2003.

19 Cheryl L. Toner, "Political Aspects Influence Military Operations," May 2002, available from <http://www.afnorth.nato.int/northern_star/ns_may_2002/ns_may_2002_article6.htm>, accessed 13 October 2003.

20. Ibid.

21. Margret H. Belknap, "The CNN Effect: Strategic Enabler or Operational Risk?" *Parameters: US Army War College*, Fall 2002. 105.

22. Douglas V. Johnson II, "The Impact of the Media on National Security Policy Decision Making", (Carlisle: Strategic Studies Institute, 1994), 17.

23. Ibid.

BIBLIOGRAPHY

Al-Haifi, Hassan, "Srebrenicia, Qana and Jenin," Focus Yemen Times, 17-28 April, 2002, available from <http://www.yementimes.com/02/iss17/focus. htm>, accessed 23 November 2003.

"Battle of Mogadishu," Wikipedia The Free Encyclopedia, available from <http://en.wikipedia.org/wiki/October_3_1993_Battle_of_Mogadishu>, assessed 10 February 2004.

Belknap, Margret H., "The CNN Effect: Strategic Enabler or Operational Risk?" Parameters: US Army War College, Fall 2002. 105.

Brown, Robin, " Clausewitz in the Age of Al-Jazeera: Rethinking the Military-Media Relationship,"available from <http://www.apsanet.org/~polcomm/ APSA%20Papers/Brown.pdf>, accessed 12 October, 2003.

Bruner, Gary P., "Military-Media Relations in Recent U.S. Operations," 14 November 1997, available from <http://www.amsc.belvoir.army.mil/military. htm>, accessed 10 February 2004.

Burns, Alex, "The Worldflash of A Coming Future," M/C Journal, available from <http://www.media-culture.org.au/0304/08-worldflash.html>, accessed 16 November, 2003.

Burns, Alex, "Weapons of Mass Protection" War Reportage and Information Society, 11 March, 2003, available from <http://www.disinfo.com/archive/ pages/article/id1298/pg1/>, accessed 20 November, 2003.

Cate, Fred H,. "CNN effect, is not clear cut," Humanitarian Affairs Review, Summer 2002,available from <http://www.globalpolicy.org/ngos/aid/2002/ summercnn.htm>, accessed 13 October, 2003.

Chossudovsky, Michel, "Iraq-War/Media-Manipulation," 10 June, 2003, available from<http://belfium.indymedia.org/news/2003/06/67527.php>, accessed 19 November, 2003.

Hulme, Simon J. MAJ., "The Modern Media: The Impact on Foreign Policy," MMAS Thesis, U.S. Army Command and General Staff College, June 1992.

"Information Warfare and Deterrence," Chapter 4. Workshop Insights and Conclusions, available from <http://www.ndu.edu/inss/books/Books%20-%201996/Information%20Warfare%20>, 19 November, 2003.

Johnson, Douglas V. II, "The Impact of the Media on National Security Policy Decision Making", (Carlisle: Strategic Studies Institute, 1994), 3.

Lafferty, Haywood, klincar, Monteith, Strednansky, "The Impact of Media Information on Enemy Effectiveness: A Model for Conflict," Proteus, A Journal of Ideas, Spring 1994, pp 1-41.

Linder, Douglas, "The My Lai Courts-Martial 1970," Famous American Trials, 1999, available from <http://www.law.umkc.edu/faculty/projects/ftrials/mylai/mylai.htm; accessed 23 November, 2002.

Muller, Kerstin, "The CNN effect, media and global governance," Speech by Minister of State Kerstin Muller to Open the Forum Global Issues on 20 February 2003, available from <http://www.auswaertiges-amt.de/www/en/ausgabe_archiv?archiv_id=4117>, accessed 16 November, 2003.

"Operation Urgent Fury," FAS Military Analysis Network, 27 May 1999, available from <http://www.fas.org/man/dod-101/ops/urgent_fury.htm>, assessed 10 February 2004.

Parenti, Michael, "Methods of Media Manipulation," available from <http://saif_w.tripod.com/america/media_manipulation.htm>, accessed on 19 November, 2003.

Project #4, "CNN Military Information," available from <http://www.louisville.edu/~rdceba01/proj4.html>, accessed 13 October, 2003.

Ricks, Charles W. "The Military-News Media Relationship: Thinking Forward" (Carlisle: Strategic Studies Institute, 1 December, 1993)

Robinson, Piers, "The CNN Effect: The Myth of News Media, Foreign Policy and Intervention," July 2002, available from <http://www.frontlist.com/detail/041529053>, accessed 16 November 2003.

Rowan Scarborough, "Accused Army Officer Gets Support," The Washington Times, October 2003, available from <http://washingtontimes.com/national/20031029-105110-6224>, accessed 23 November 2003.

Shahar, Yael, "Information Warfare: The Perfect Terrorist Weapon," available from http://www.ict.org.il/articles/infowar.htm; accessed 19 November, 2003.

Stockwell, David B., Major, "Press Coverage in Somalia," available from <http://www.globalsecurity.org/military/library/report/1995/SDB.htm>, accessed 10 February 2004.

"The Mass Media's Impact on International Affairs," U.S. Institute of Peace Watch, June 1997, available from http://www.usip.org/peacewatch/1997/697/media.html; accessed 17 November, 2003.

Toner, Cheryl L., "Political Aspects Influence Military Operations," May 2002, available from http://www.afnorth.nato.int/northern_star/ns_may_2002/ns_may_2002_article6.htm; internet; accessed 13 October, 2003.

Venable, Barry E., MAJ. USA, "66 The Amy and the Media," Military Review, Jan-Feb 2002, available from http://www-cgsc.army.mil/milrev/english/JanFeb02/venable.asp; accessed 6 November 2003.

Wereldomreop, "Psychological Warfare Against Iraq." Radio Netherlands, available frommhttp://www.rnw.nl/realradio/features/html/iraq-psywar.html; accessed 19 November, 2003.

CHAPTER 3

EMBEDDED MEDIA: FAILED TEST OR THE FUTURE OF MILITARY-MEDIA RELATIONS?

Lieutenant Colonel Michael J. Oehl
United States Marine Corps

The Military View? *"Four hostile newspapers are more to be feared than a thousand bayonets"*
                                                                —Napoleon

The Media View? *"War is a drug...it is peddled by myth makers, historians, war correspondents, filmmakers, novelists and the state...."*
                                                                – Chris Hedges
                                                (War is a Force That Gives Us Meaning)

INTRODUCTION

The relationship between the United States military and the media has been a complex one for years. Like any relationship, it can be characterized by ebbs and flows, good times and bad, from the perspective of both institutions. From Vietnam to Operation Iraqi Freedom (OIF), the military-media relationship's complexity has been the result of a clash of cultures. The glaring philosophical differences between the two institutions make them unlikely bedfellows. The military is a fundamentally closed society; arguably more conservative than most American institutions. It is accountable to civilian leadership within the United States government, and its mission focus is on the protection of American interests. The media by comparison is considerably more liberal. It is, with few exceptions, privately owned and accountable to stockholders with a mission of reporting newsworthy events that will either sell newspapers, magazines, or airtime for a monetary profit. The goal of the American media is to write or present an intriguing story. That "attention-getter" translates to money. The military, by contrast, is not a profit making entity. It exists solely because the American public wants it to exist due to a perceived need for protection from those that would do the country harm. It is an institution funded by tax-paying Americans that does not provide a service to the country that is easily quantifiable. This places it in a sensitive position: its competence can be proved to the American public only on rare opportunities. Those opportunities, more often than not, come during times of conflict. Furthermore, its success or failure reflects not only on the military as an institution but also on the administration that made the decision to use military force. The irony of this relationship is that one institution is committed to defending the Constitution of the United States, the very document that allows the other institution to ply its trade. Both are fundamental to American democracy. Despite that ironic link, the military and the media continue to have a love-hate relationship. This paper will attempt to explore that relationship, as it has existed from Vietnam through Operation Iraqi Freedom (OIF), while identifying the causes for such a relationship and what it means for the future.

VIETNAM

This history of clashing cultures precedes Vietnam, but one could argue that the challenges apparent in the relationship have not changed much. This analysis will address the relationship as it evolved from that period. Additionally, for clarity, the definition of the relationship cannot always be narrowed to the military. Those governmental institutions that provide the military its marching orders, the Executive Branch of government and the Department of Defense (DoD), often affect it. Therefore, any fair assessment of a relationship between the media and the military will include the influence of such governmental institutions. Although the cultural differences between the media and the military are significant, the relationship is affected at times by tangible and often interpersonal events. In any commitment of military force, the United States Government eventually comes to the crossroads of having to justify, or at least explain, such a commitment to the American people. The avenue for such an explanation inevitably runs through the media. This reality held true during Vietnam, when President Lyndon Johnson's administration ordered an increase in American military involvement. As the conflict in Vietnam escalated from the perspective of a greater commitment of manpower, the Johnson administration found itself in a position where it had to justify such escalation. Unfortunately, when it turned to the media to present the administration's part of the story, it turned to an institution that was becoming increasingly frustrated with the administration and its apparent disdain for the media. The perception of the media was that the Johnson administration failed to treat them with respect. This was especially evident in the White House Press Corps, where reporters felt that they were not treated as human beings and that there was no consideration for the reporters as people with lives of their own. By relying on routine last-minute announcements of press conferences, the administration hampered their travel and personal plans. It left them tied to the White House Press Room, unable to make plans of their own. This process bred contempt, as the press considered themselves targets of an administration bent on secrecy. This outlook clouded their perception of how the President handled Vietnam.[1] Johnson and his advisors were astute enough to realize that they needed the media to tell their side of the story. With five thousand reporters from sixty countries covering the war at different times, they had no choice but to attempt to get their arms around the media, lest the story get told in a less than flattering way.[2]

During the spring of 1967, Johnson made attempts to endear himself to the media, perhaps subscribing to Sun Tzu's theory that, "to know your enemy, you must become your enemy...keep your friends close and your enemies closer." He became more forthcoming and invited key correspondents to the White House for social gatherings.[3] This tactic appeared to pay dividends for the President, as a noted reporter who lost a son in Vietnam in 1966, Merriman Smith, mentioned at a breakfast he was attending that he felt "Johnson had been treated unfairly by the press—worse than he'd seen in 25 years of covering the White House."[4] Unfortunately, the honeymoon was short-lived. Soon Johnson was reported commenting "about sympathizing with those who would chloroform reporters, and that some reporters would rather drink hemlock than accept the truth of some of his statistics." These comments turned the press against him again.[5] Rather than attempt to repair a failing relationship, the President lashed out. "Counted among those doubters and gloom spreaders, in Johnson's tally, were the members of the media. Unfortunately, a student carrying a sign or a protestor wearing a beard, or an attention-seeker burning a draft card in front of a camera can get more attention—and more billing—than all 10,000 of these volunteers" (referring to the military stationed in Vietnam).[6]

This relationship degenerated as time went on, with the administration continuing to present an appearance of secrecy while the media was more aggressively questioning the methodology of the President and his closest advisors. Consequently, Johnson was unable to clearly communicate his vision of victory in Vietnam through the press to the American public. As a result, journalists' support for the war declined, and they reflected their dismay in the articles they wrote.

The contentious relationship was not resident solely within the beltway. The President's ranking military officer in Vietnam, General William Westmoreland, had his own struggles with making the media/military relationship work. Despite early attempts to enhance the relationship by improving the flow of information to reporters by frequent press conferences, the relationship declined as more reporters arrived in Vietnam as a result of troop increase through 1965.[7] As the involvement of U.S. troops increased, commanders became concerned about the potential for reporters to release sensitive operational information. In the early part of 1965, General Westmoreland explored the possibility of censoring the press. The growing number of reporters in the country made that option remote. It was ultimately decided that any release of sensitive information would result in a correspondent's loss of press credentials.[8] The end result of this "voluntary restraint" was a freedom on the part of the press never before experienced in a war zone.

The press in Vietnam had relatively free access. That access presented a challenge for Westmoreland, as the relationship between his civilian leaders and the media deteriorated. As operations began, the relationship was generally strong. When things soured, negative stories made the papers and airwaves. The military and administration, hyper-sensitive about negative war publicity, lost what little trust they had in the media, effectively throwing fuel on a fire that was already beginning to burn out of control.

As the administration wrestled with the challenge of getting its side of the story out through an increasingly suspicious media, the news rolled on with stories influenced less by governmental input. Throughout the decline of the relationship, Americans and the media became more aligned in their view of the war. Their shared skepticism was driven by the feeling that they were uninformed, that the United States Government was keeping something from them.[9]

As he addressed the operational issues on the ground, General Westmoreland was undoubtedly influenced by his Commander-In-Chief's view of the media. Evidence of this can be seen in comments made to Westmoreland during a visit to Johnson's ranch after he was out of office. Johnson commented to Westmoreland that "...early in the war he should have proposed press censorship, no matter how complex the problems that might have generated."[10] This is an indicator of how extensively the relationship had degenerated and the real level of distrust that defined the administration's view of the media. Furthermore, the timing of this comment, after Johnson's departure from government service, speaks volumes about the emotional impact the strained relationship had on the president.

In the summer of 1967, a Gallup Poll revealed that sixty-five percent of Americans felt the administration was not telling them all they should know about Vietnam. Vietnam, in essence, became a turning point with regard to press passivity. During previous wars, the press generally deferred to the United States Government with regard to information passed on regarding military issues. As the consensus on foreign policy began to disintegrate during Vietnam, journalists began to question that deference. The media became aware that a government under pressure will not always speak the truth.[11] This issue would have longstanding negative implications for future military-media relations and lies at the very core of the tension that has existed between the media and the military since Vietnam.

As support for the war waned, the Johnson administration's attempt to repair the damage was met with distrust by a media that was engaged in reporting on the ground, often embedded with units. The media was seeing through what they perceived to be the "spin" of the administration, since they were seeing a different Vietnam on the ground than the administration was reporting. The Tet Offensive of 1968 drove the point home through the media that the Johnson administration was being less than truthful in its claims that the American military was making significant progress towards winning the war.[12]

Westmoreland's many challenges dealing with the press can be seen by comments in his memoirs that Vietnam was "the first war in history lost in the columns of the New York Times."[13] Westmoreland was, in some ways, the recipient of the media's wrath with the administration. Instead of human-interest stories, the focus, over time, shifted to reports of failures of the service's rifle (the M-16), poor morale amongst troops, and criticism of the South Vietnamese government.[14]

Those in the military and the media affected by the relationships that were born in the fields of Vietnam often went on to assume more influential positions within their respective institutions. Reporters in the field, like their military counterparts, were elevated to leadership positions within major news bureaus. They carried their experiences with them as they moved up the organization ladder. Those experiences were often based on a significant amount of distrust. Westmoreland's contention, that the war was "lost in the columns of the New York Times" was not a unique opinion among military leaders or the administration that endorsed their involvement in Vietnam. The end result of this dynamic was a relationship built on distrust.

This contentious relationship can be traced to vast cultural differences between the media and the military. It is summed up well by Melissa Healy, a Los Angeles Times reporter who covered the Pentagon:

> I began to recognize that I was operating, for all practical purposes, as a foreign correspondent. I was dipping into a world with a language of its own, with a society of its own that, in every respect paralleled U.S. civil society. But it paralleled it; it was not part of it. It was separate. It had its own justice system, its own retail system, its own health-care system. Everything was different. It's really important to have reporters who can be on the beat long enough to understand that....It's a culture of conservatives and of careerism in the military that sees no potential investment in talking to reporters, that truly sees no benefit to one's career. The point is that you can find few, if any, career military people who can conceive that talking to a reporter not only is in the normal line of responsibility to taxpayers, but that it could ever be of any benefit to them. They can only see the possibility that it could hurt their careers. It's a deeply, deeply inbred attitude.[15]

The opinions of Ms. Healy certainly proved prophetic as the United States moved from Vietnam into other conflicts around the globe, namely Grenada, Panama, and Desert Storm. The classic clash of cultures stemming from the obvious differences between the media and the military is striking and can be linked to challenges in each of these conflicts. The media as an institution is trained to be skeptical of authority, while those in the military are expected to respect authority. Journalists generally relish their individualism, while their military counterparts are so disciplined that they appear to have sacrificed their individuality. The media see eccentricity as having its own utility, while those in uniform are more likely to reject "out of the box" behavior. Given these divergent cultural positions, it should be no surprise that the two institutions have had differing opinions through the years.[16]

GRENADA

Despite the palpable tension that continued to exist between the media and the military, public affairs personnel were not involved in the planning for Grenada. As the invasion progressed in 1983, the media made multiple attempts to cover the operation. Nearly six hundred reporters from various news agencies arrived on Barbados as the operation began, hoping to cover the invasion. Surprised commanders, having not planned for any media intervention, effectively stiff-armed the media, keeping them away from the area of operations for two days. Journalists that were resourceful enough to make it to the island were detained by the military.[17] Unfortunately, from the perspective of military-media relations, the lack of media access only served to heighten suspicions that the Pentagon was hiding something.[18] Grenada infuriated the press and caused them to exert a great deal of pressure on DoD in order to preclude a reoccurrence of such an incident. The inability of the press to effectively cover the Grenada invasion, and their subsequent appeal to the Pentagon's leadership, resulted in then Chairman of the Joint Chiefs of Staff, General John Vessey, convening the Sidle Commission to investigate the best way to ensure access is afforded the media in future conflicts. The end result of this commission was the establishment of the DoD National Media Pool (DNMP).[19] On the surface, the commission's recommendations appeared to be a viable first step towards allowing greater, and timelier, media access to military operations. The new arrangement would allow a representative pool of journalists and photographers, representing all aspects of the media, to report back from a given conflict's area of operations to a centralized military headquarters.[20]

PANAMA

One unintended result of the DNMP's establishment was that military commanders believed the organization would take care of itself without significant involvement of the military chain of command. This approach proved disastrous for an already strained relationship as the United States planned and executed the invasion of Panama in 1989. The Pentagon delayed sending its "pool" of reporters from Washington. Instead, non-pool reporters made their way to Panama on their own to cover the invasion. Those chosen for the job, and sanctioned by DoD, arrived late and developed reports off of prepared DoD briefings and CNN reports from those reporters that were independent of the pool.[21] Hence, the invasion of Panama saw the failure of the DNMP. Left on their own, reporters without the necessary support from commanders required to operate within Panama, were only able to cover the later stages of the operation.[22] The Pentagon did little to demonstrate good will towards the media, and the new CJCS, General Colin Powell, was compelled to put the word out to commanders that he expected their personal involvement with respect to public affairs planning and execution.[23]

A greater emphasis was placed on Public Affairs planning after the CJCS articulated his guidance. However, the propensity of the media to cover less-than-flattering stories would keep the relationship strained up through Desert Storm. Whether it was covering military shortcomings in the way of sex scandals or cost overruns of weapons systems, the media was in search of a story. Unfortunately, that "story" was often at the expense of career military personnel. The result of this unique arrangement was a military that remained distrustful of the media. This was a military that, as Ms. Healy wrote, saw "no potential investment in talking to reporters, that truly sees no benefit to one's career."

The failure of the Pentagon to effectively balance its desire to assuage the media with its need for a coherent media strategy was a nagging thorn in the side of military-media relations. The media was growing increasingly frustrated as it was promised access that was never delivered.

DESERT SHIELD/STORM

As the Pentagon found itself planning to push the Iraqi military from Kuwait in 1990, a concerted effort was made by the Pentagon and the media to facilitate coverage of any developing conflict. In a continuing effort to repair the relationship with the press, the Pentagon activated the seventeen-member DNMP at the beginning of Operation Desert Shield. Despite the Pentagon's good intentions, Saudi restrictions on granting visas to reporters stymied the pool. Faced with another Panama fiasco, many reporters decided to fly into Bahrain and find their own way to Saudi Arabia.[24]

And senior military leaders remained suspicious of the media. These suspicions, coupled with improvements in technology that allowed for more rapid transmission of stories, set the stage for another contentious military-media showdown. The Commander, U.S. Central Command, General Norman Schwarzkopf, was a Vietnam veteran. It is not too much of an intellectual leap to assume that General Schwarzkopf harbored some ill feelings towards the media from his time as a young officer in Vietnam. Evidence of this was his desire for a controlled press rather than a workable pool arrangement. "Veterans of Vietnam, they remembered not that war was messy but that news accounts made the military look inept. They had no intention of letting reporters have a clear view of the battlefield."[25] Retired Lieutenant General Bernard Trainor, U.S. Marine Corps, believes there is some truth to this Vietnam bias. However, he concluded that the real fallout from this passing of the torch was a new generation of military officers that does not trust the media. "It is a legacy of the war, and it takes root soon after they enter service. Like racism, anti-Semitism, and all forms of bigotry, it is irrational but nonetheless real. The credo of the military seems to have become 'duty, honor, country, and hate the media.'"[26] It appears to be this credo that permeated the relationship between the media and the military during the Gulf War. As a result, the military in the Gulf was successful at "managing" the media that were sent to Saudi Arabia to cover the war. Ironically, the very way it was managed by different services appears to have redefined the relationship for future conflicts.

It was generally believed by the different services that the Army and Navy eschewed a golden opportunity to tell their story, while the Marine

Corps could never get enough media people in the field to cover their units.[27] While General Schwarzkopf was restricting interviews to those reporters he liked, and Army commanders were only grudgingly accepting journalists assigned to them, Lieutenant General Walter Boomer, former Marine Corps Public Affairs Officer and the senior Marine Corps commander in the Gulf War, pushed for more journalists even as the war kicked off. John Fialka states; "The differences between the two services' skills at handling public affairs were so vast that reporters sometimes wondered whether they represented different countries."[28]

The Navy also forfeited a big opportunity in the Gulf War by allowing every ship commander the option of deciding whether or not he wanted media coverage. Although the media desired to cover battleship involvement in the war, the commander of the USS Iowa refused to allow media on his ship. Although the Iowa was a significant supporter of the offensive effort through Naval Gunfire support of ground maneuver, its actions and those of its crew never received media coverage.[29]

In contrast, America witnessed many minutes of video, provided by the Air Force, of precision-guided munitions striking their intended targets, as well as footage of Marine Corps units arriving on the outskirts of Kuwait City. What was largely missed were the largest tank battles since World War II, because of the Army's reluctance to allow media to go along during 7th Corps' attack. Although never quantified, it could be argued that the inability of Americans to see the relative value of the Army's contribution to the Gulf War could only hurt when the service competes for its share of a limited Defense Department budget.

OPERATION IRAQI FREEDOM

In the thirteen years between Desert Storm and OIF, the military appears to have come to the conclusion, at least temporarily, that it needs the media. Although the media has no legal right to force its way onto the battlefield, the American people are not likely to tolerate a military that operates under a veil of secrecy. So, despite vast cultural differences, the military, as the controller of access to the battlefield, allowed the media unprecedented access to its operations as it set the stage for overthrowing the Iraqi regime. The interesting dynamic that defined embedded media during OIF reveals a continuing culture clash that will likely forever define the military-media relationship.

The media had unprecedented access to military operations during OIF. The term "embedded," although in existence long before OIF, became the defining word with regard to the media's coverage of the conflict in Iraq. Despite this unfettered access, the future of the relationship between those who fight the Nation's battles and those who report on those battles remains in question. Countless articles published before, during, and after OIF judged the embedded media program as flawed. Embedding was said to skew the objectivity of the reporters assigned to units; it was called a propaganda ploy on behalf of the Pentagon. Embedded reporters, these commentators said, could not be trusted because they were "in bed" with the military. *Poynteronline* interviewed Chris Hedges, an accomplished war correspondent with experience in El Salvador, Kosovo, and the Persian Gulf just before the ground offensive of OIF. During the interview, he identified his perception of the flaws of the embedded media program. Some of these point directly to the inexperience of the reporters that were embedded with units. He cited the fact that these reporters would be dependent on the military for everything, and he claimed that they would not want to get very near actual combat; which, he said, was something that the military would "be all too willing to oblige."[30] Part of this statement is true; namely, that the majority of embedded reporters had no experience covering combat operations. However, the latter part of Hedge's opinion is flawed.

Despite the lack of the reporters' combat experience, my personal experience with five embedded reporters showed a genuine willingness to cover the most direct combat. In fact, as a battalion commander, I usually tried to appease my five embeds, who all wanted to be with the first unit in contact. Because of their willingness to confront the dangers associated with combat, they developed a close relationship with the Marines with whom they moved. This relationship was predictable in that it is no secret that human beings who share a traumatic experience together tend to bond emotionally. All of my embeds developed personal relationships with the Marines of 2d Tank Battalion, relationships that would continue after the war. Despite the new-found relationships, two of my embedded reporters, Mike Cerre of ABC News Nightline, and Jim Landers, of the Dallas Morning News, were not only able to witness the horrors of war, but were given the "green light" to report about whatever they saw. Cerre reported at length for ABC on 2d Tank Battalion's involvement in a five-hour firefight and an incident involving civilian casualties during the evening of 4 April 2003. At no time was he ever restrained with regard to reporting on the command, despite the nature of the subject matter. Cerre comments:

> On the same day that ammo dump blew, I was involved in probably the worst nightmare for the Department of Defense concerning the embed process because I was right there when this civilian tragedy happened. The incident started when a civilian vehicle tried to come through the checkpoint and ignored the warning shots. The Marines opened fire to try and disable the vehicle – which they did. Two people were killed in that vehicle and in the backseat were women and children who were wounded.... I looked up and saw the headlights of a truck. I could hear it accelerating. The Marines opened fire on it and disabled the driver. The truck careened, hit a dirt mound on the side of the road, flipped over on its side, and went right over our heads. It crashed maybe fifty feet beyond us. It was a dump truck that was beige with military painting and had military colored stripes on the radiator. The driver had an AK47 and a set of uniforms in a duffle bag in the back of the truck. But following right behind was an agricultural truck and a minibus filled with civilians. The Marines opened fire on all the vehicles as they came through the checkpoint. They killed three children and two women on the bus. Because I had such an open relationship with the unit, they knew I was going to have to make this report.[31]

The media covering the war for the 2d Tank Battalion were given seamless access to the command's Marines as well as the story of combat as it unfolded, with little influence from the commander. Mike Cerre was the first reporter to transmit live from a ground combat unit as the battalion crossed the border into Iraq from Kuwait during the early evening hours of 19 March 2003. His timely story, portrayed to ABC News' Peter Jennings back in the states, was made possible by a commander that allowed him to report whatever he wanted, as long as it was accurate and did not compromise operational security. Jim Landers and Cheryl Diaz-Meyers, reporter and photographer for the Dallas Morning News, had the same access Cerre had. Landers wrote an article on the incident Cerre described above, and Diaz-Meyers photographed the scene. The article was published on 6 April 2003, describing the incident with the same detail as Cerre:

> They carried the bodies of the children out first. There was a girl of about 12, whom the Marines wrapped in her black abaya cloak. Next off the shattered minibus was her brother, a boy of about 4, whom the Marines covered in a sports jacket. A sister, about 6 years old, had fallen between the seats. They placed her beside her siblings on a blanket.[32]

Before releasing the article, Landers asked me to take a look at it, not because he was required to, but as a professional courtesy. I reviewed it without any intent of debating what we knew to be the facts at the time. No Marine, if given the choice, would have wanted to see either Cerre's or Lander's stories get aired or published. The Marines were not proud of what happened that evening, but it was what it was. It was the ugly side of war, and the reporters reported it.

CONCLUSION

The military-media relationship has evolved over the years, driven largely by a desire on the part of the media establishment to open the door into a society that it feels is too secretive, a society that they may never truly understand. It is likely that the process of embedding media will continue in future conflicts. The proverbial cat is out of the bag, and any attempt to put it back in is likely to result in the Pentagon getting "clawed" by the media. For the Pentagon leadership, it has become a "damned if you do, damned if you don't" scenario. After being criticized by the media for not providing enough access to combat, they now find themselves as the subject of criticism for allowing a level of access that is "too close," so close that it skews the objectivity of journalists that stake their professional reputations on their ability to remain detached from the subjects they cover.

The idea of embedding reporters with combat units must have been seen as a media utopia to those making the decisions within news organizations around the United States. However, criticism of embedded media continues to focus on the lack of objectivity of the reporters that lived with, and reported on, the servicemen with whom they were embedded. A number of renowned journalists have voiced their opinions that the Pentagon is skewing the view of war that Americans are seeing.

Both Morley Safer and Andy Rooney, of 60 Minutes fame, are skeptics. "They called Vietnam 'McNamara's War'", says Morley Safer in reference the former defense secretary. This is Rumsfeld's war—and he seems to be managing it far better than McNamara did. The operative word is 'managed.'" Mr. Rooney stated, "It's very difficult to write anything critical about a guy you're going to have breakfast with the next morning. Ernie Pyle didn't write any stories about cowards in World War II, even though there were some. I suspect in this war, we're going to get a lot of stories about heroes."[33] These sentiments were not uncommon with regard to discussions about the embedded media program. Despite viewership being up (three hundred percent for the cable news channels and ten percent overall) for broadcasts since March 19, skeptics were readily available. Marvin Kalb, a senior fellow at Harvard University's Shorenstein Center on the Press, stated, "If a reporter is with a soldier, sleeps in the same tent, eats the same food, faces roughly the same danger—if the reporter is a human being, it is very difficult to…write critical copy about the guy he just had dinner with."[34] These negative comments on the objectivity of embedded media are ironic. These same commentators would likely have argued for greater access to military operations had there been no embedded media program.

A generation of combat veterans, both military and media, evolved from the experience of OIF. The process of embedding media served to break down some of the preconceived notions and prejudices that the military and media industries had towards one another by educating both sides on the duties and responsibilities of the other. The shared experiences of military members and the reporters embedded with them should ultimately result in a better understanding of not only why a relationship is necessary but how such a relationship can be mutually beneficial to both camps. It is for this reason that the process of embedding media with military units should continue as a method to allay the natural distrust found between two institutions with such vast cultural differences. Nonetheless, the ongoing debate on the success or failure of the program points to a future relationship that is destined to be fraught with tension, despite the concessions made by both sides.

ENDNOTES

1. Kathleen J. Thurman, *Lyndon Johnson's Dual War: Vietnam and the Press* (Chicago: The University of Chicago Press, 1985), 9.

2. David Lamb, *Vietnam Now: A Reporter Returns* (New York: Public Affairs, 2002), 10.

3. Thurman, 180.

4. Ibid., 179.

5. Ibid., 181.

6. Ibid., 186.

7. Lauren B. Thompson, ed., *Defense Beat: The Dilemmas of Defense Coverage* (New York, NY: Lexington Books, 1991), 41.

8. Ibid., 42.

9. Thurman, 190.

10. William C. Westmoreland, *A Soldier Reports* (Garden City, NY: Garden City Press, 1976), 386.

11. Daniel C. Hallin, *The Uncensored War: The Media and Vietnam* (New York, NY. Oxford University Press, 1986), 63.

12. Ibid., 43.

13. Ibid., 10.

14. Thurman, 42.

15. Frank Aukofer and William Lawrence, *America's Team: A Report on the Relationship Between the Media and the Military* (Nashville, TN: The Freedom Forum First Amendment Center, 1995), 83.

16. Nancy Ethiel, series editor. *The Catigney Conference Series. Reporting The Next War.* (Wheaton, Ill. Catigney, 1992), 11.

17. Johanna Neuman, *Lights Camera War* p 206.

18. Ibid.

19. Ankofer p 44.

20. Neuman p 207.

21. Ibid., p 208.

22. Aukofer and Lawrence, 4.

23. Ibid., 44.

24. Douglas Porch, "Media/Military Relations in the United States,"

available from <http://www/pdgs.org/porch.htm>. Internet; accessed 29 January 2004.

25. Johanna Neuman, *Lights, Camera, War* (New York, NY: St. Martin's Press), 208.

26. Hedrich Smith, ed. *The Media and the Gulf War* (Washington D.C.: Seven Locks Press, 1992), 69.

27. Fialka, 27.

28. Ibid., 26.

29. Nancy Ethiel, series editor. *The Catigney Conference Series. The Military and the Media: Facing the Future* (Wheaton, Ill. Catigney, 1998), 39.

30. Robin Sloan, interviewer "Chris Hedges on War and the Press," available from <http://www.poynter.org/content/content_print. asp?id=25166&custom= >. Internet: accessed 21 Nov 2003.

31. Bill Katovsky and Timothy Carlson, *Embedded: The Media at War in Iraq, an Oral History* (Guilford, Connecticut: The Lyons Press, 2003), 96.

32. Jim Landers, "A horrible night at a roadblock. Trying to flee Baghdad, they met disaster," available from <http://www/pozar.com/ Ky%20site/kyblog.html>. Internet: accessed 16 February 2004.

33. Peter Johnson, "Reporters go along with military Upbeat stories play well at home, but critics see skewed view of war," available from <http://usatoday.com/usatonline/20030326/4991525s.htm>. Internet; accessed 11 November 2003.

34. David Hiltbrand and Gail Shister, "A flood of images into homes," available from <http://www.philly.com/mld/inquirer/news/nation/5490137. htm>. Internet; accessed 11 November 2003.

BIBLIOGRAPHY

Aukofer, Frank, and William Lawrence. *America's Team: A Report on the Relationship Between the Media and the Military*. Nashville, TN: The Freedom Forum First Amendment Center, 1995.

Beaubien, Michael P., and John S. Wyeth, Jr. eds. *Views on the News: The Media and Public Opinion*. New York, NY: New York University Press, 1994.

Ethiel, Nancy, series editor. *The Catigney Conference Series. Reporting The Next War*. Wheaton, Ill. Catigney, 1992.

Ethiel, Nancy, series editor. *The Catigney Conference Series. The Military and the Media: Facing the Future*. Wheaton, Ill. Catigney, 1998.

Fialka, John J. *Hotel Warriors: Covering the Gulf War*. Washington, D.C.: The Woodrow Wilson Center Press, 1991.

Hallin, Daniel C. *The Uncensored War: The Media and Vietnam*. New York, NY. Oxford University Press, 1986.

Hedges, Chris. *War is a Force That Gives Us Meaning*. New York, NY: Public Affairs, 2002.

Hiltbrand, David and Gail Shister, "A flood of images into homes," 27 March 2003; available from <http://www.philly.com/mld/inquirer/news/nation/5490137.htm>. Internet. Accessed 11 November 2003.

Johnson, Peter, "Reporters Go Along With Military Upbeat Stories Play Well At Home, But Critics See Skewed View Of War," 26 March 2003; available from <http://usatoday.com/usatonline/20030326/4991525s.htm>. Internet. Accessed 11 November 2003.

Katovsky, Bill and Timothy Carlson, *Embedded: The Media at War in Iraq, an Oral History*. Guilford, Connecticut: The Lyons Press, 2003.

Lamb, David. *Vietnam Now: A Reporter Returns*. New York: Public Affairs, 2002.

Land, Nathaniel. *Dispatches From The Front*. New York, NY: Henry Holland Company, Inc., 1995.

Landers, Jim, "A horrible night at a roadblock. Trying to flee Baghdad, they met disaster," available from <http://www/pozar.com/Ky%20site/kyblog.html >. Internet: accessed 16 February 2004.

Neuman, Johanna. *Lights, Camera, War*. New York, NY: St. Martin's Press, 1996.

Porch, Douglas, "Media/Military Relations in the United States," July 2001; available from <http://www/pdgs.org/porch.htm>. Internet. Accessed 29 January 2004.

Schudson, Michael. *The Power of News*. Cambridge, MA: Harvard University Press, 1995.

Sloan, Robin, interviewer "Chris Hedges on War and the Press," 19 March 2003; available from <http://www.poynter.org/content/content_print. asp?id=25166&custom=>. Internet. Accessed 21 Nov 2003.

Smith, Hedrich, ed. *The Media and the Gulf War*. Washington D.C.: Seven Locks Press, 1992.

Thompson, Lauren B. (ed.). *Defense Beat: The Dilemmas of Defense Coverage*. New York, NY: Lexington Books, 1991.

Thurman, Kathleen J. *Lyndon Johnson's Dual War: Vietnam and the Press*. Chicago: The University of Chicago Press, 1985.

Westmoreland, William C. *A Soldier Reports*. Garden City, NY 1976.

CHAPTER 4

EMBEDDING SUCCESS INTO THE MILITARY-
MEDIA RELATIONSHIP

Commander Jose L. Rodriguez
United States Naval Reserve

The lessons learned and commentaries regarding the Defense Department's media embedded reporter policy and resulting coverage of Operation Iraqi Freedom (OIF) are still being written. It is clear that the wider use of embedded reporters provided the world an unprecedented view of combat and of the warfighters. This state-of-the-art view brought the public real-time images, sounds, and soldiering via gyroscopic satellite vehicles, videophones, cell phones, and night vision photography.

However, what exactly has this 21st century coverage provided the American public and the world? Has it provided a comprehensive, balanced, and true perspective of the prosecution of war and its effects, a higher level of journalism, or just merely "info-tainment"?[1] Or could it be the media utilizing its new technology in an attempt to fill the 24-hour news cycle and feed the public's hunger for knowledge about the war? These questions will continue to be debated by the fourth estate, academia, the military and the public.

Information is power. As one of the four elements of power in a Grand Strategy, its proper management is vital to our national interests, as stated by David Jablonsky, instructor at the U.S. Army War College, "This combination of enhanced communication and dissemination of information, however, is a two-edged sword that cuts across all the social determinants of power in national strategy."[2] With the impending battle with Iraq as part of the Global War on Terrorism, the Department of Defense was concerned with implementing a policy to counter disinformation and to disseminate international messages, a policy that would provide the media greater access to the battlefield in delivering accurate combat reports. In return DoD would be able to get out its message about a smaller, swifter, highly technical, fighting force engaged in liberating a people from the hands of a brutal and desperate dictator.

THE MILITARY-MEDIA RELATIONSHIP SINCE VIETNAM

The historic relationship between the military and the media has been a mix of cooperation and tension. Members of the fourth estate seek to obtain and report the truth, while the military seeks to control the flow of the truth. This tension, combined with the goals and unique personality traits of those called to each profession, has been cause for a multitude of disagreements and a high level of distrust.

In no other conflict was the relationship between the two more strained and distrustful than in the Vietnam conflict. This adversarial relationship during the conflict was "intensified and then institutionalized ... when the Pentagon and the press both seemed to lose respect for the mission, veracity and honor of the other side."[3]

According to William V. Kennedy in *The Media and the Military*, the roots of this conflict arose from cultural and ideological differences between those who enter the military and those who serve in the media.[4] He asserts that these differences combined with reporters' lack of knowledge of the military prior to assignment in the field resulted in uninformed or negative reporting. This reporting caused the leadership to "view these stories as a major reason they were losing the war at home while they were winning the battles in Vietnam."[5]

Following the Tet Offensive a "credibility gap" emerged, as "the disturbing images on the TV screen were in sharp contrast to the official reports that the United States was ... winning the war and would be out of Vietnam soon."[6] Negative reporting and decreasing public support led to a "lasting distrust for the press ... on the part of many, if not most, U.S. officers of all services..." which, "shorn of the pretenses necessary to maintain a workable day-to-day relationship...," was "hatred."[7]

From the conclusion of the conflict in Vietnam and throughout the next two-plus decades, journalists and military members were ingrained with enmity towards each other. Due to this bitter relationship, the military limited press access in later conflicts.[8] Two such conflicts with no or limited press access were Grenada and Panama.

In 1983, during the invasion of Grenada, there were no reporters accompanying U.S. troops. "Reporters who traveled to the island in boats were turned away at gunpoint."[9] In 1989, at the onset of the invasion of Panama, despite the Pentagon's promises to assist the press in reaching the island, hundreds of reporters were stranded in Miami, Florida, and Costa Rica.[10] As a result, "there were no pictures or eyewitness accounts of three battles the first day, in which 23 U.S. soldiers were killed and 265 wounded."[11]

For the Gulf War, the military eased the severe restrictions to access and employed a pool system. Critics noted that, "the Pentagon micromanaged coverage, setting up a pool system where specially chosen 'pool' reporters were taken to the front to gather material to share with other journalists. But the pool was never allowed to witness a battle as it unfolded."[12] John MacArthur, *Harper's* magazine publisher and author, wrote, "the government and media misled the public and that pool reporting was a 'crushing defeat' for freedom of the press."[13]

In Kosovo and during the early action in Afghanistan, both largely air campaigns with the exception of Special Forces ground units, "there was no concerted effort to put reporters near the fighting, and the press complained bitterly that the Pentagon was slow to confirm events on the ground."[14] According to the media, the pool system was not working.

Following a raid on Mullah Omar's headquarters by Army Rangers, with no pool reporter, news organizations executives were up in arms. Shortly afterward, the Navy and the Marine Corps began to embed reporters on ships and with Marine units on a trial basis. Because of the positive coverage of operations by the Marines, the Army decided to embed as well.[15]

BATTLE FOR PUBLIC OPINION PRE-OIF

Following the tragedies of September 11, 2001, U.S. and international public opinion firmly supported military engagement in retaliation against the Taliban regime in Afghanistan as part of the war against terrorism.

When public debate shifted to the question of Iraq's role in terror, U.S. policy support waned at home and internationally, including some long-standing allies. The battle lines were drawn between those who supported toppling Hussein preemptively to eliminate the growing threat of Iraq's possession of weapons of mass destruction, and those who opposed invading a sovereign nation with a duly-elected president who had neither attacked nor threatened a neighboring country.

The battle for public opinion was debated in all available media: print, television, radio, and the internet. Much of U.S. opinion favored action against Iraq, while much of the international community opposed it. Adding to the anti-invasion fervor was incendiary, anti-U.S. reporting by Al-Jazeera, the Qatar-based satellite network that broadcasts throughout the Arabic-language region.

With United Nations resolutions, U.S. ultimatums, and deadlines drawing near, the Department of Defense faced the distinct prospect of fighting a U.S.-led coalition of willing countries against an Arabic-speaking nation in an unpopular war. For the United States to exercise informational power in the impending crisis, a different strategy would have to be employed. This strategy would leverage the media in accurately depicting the coalition military and the compassionate actions of liberation. This could only be accomplished in cooperation with the media, whose members had vocalized discontent at military-media relations for quite some time. It would be necessary to devise a media policy that would strike a balance between the relatively unfettered access and reporting in Vietnam and the severe restrictions of Grenada, Panama, and the Gulf War. Enter Victoria Clarke, Assistant Secretary of Defense for Public Affairs, and her Deputy Secretary, Bryan Whitman, a former Army officer.

EMBEDDED MEDIA POLICY

In October 2002, Clarke and Whitman developed a plan to assign or "embed" reporters with the troops. Limited embedding was tried in limited usage with around forty reporters in Afghanistan during Operation Enduring Freedom in response to media objections that they had no access to the battlefield. Clarke's embed vision would be "dramatically different in scope and numbers than anything tried before."[16]

Whitman voiced the objectives for DoD's media policy: "to neutralize the disinformation efforts of our adversaries ... we wanted to build and maintain support for U.S. policy as well as achieve information dominance. We wanted to be able to demonstrate the professionalism of the U.S. military."[17]

Assistant Secretary Clarke, in a briefing of the policy to public affairs officers, stated that the strategy was to "expose audiences to the complete picture:

- Show combat, humanitarian, and coalition ops
- Demonstrate commitment to avoid civilian casualties
- Make the case against Hussein – his intent to develop and use WMD; record of torture and oppression
- Preempt Iraqi attacks by demonstrating past behavior
- Rapidly respond & refute Iraqi charges
- Facilitate robust media access

   o To counter likely Iraqi lies and distortions
   o To highlight professionalism of U.S. forces."[18]

The embedding plan would assign more than six hundred reporters at a ratio of eighty percent U.S. reporters to twenty percent non-U.S. reporters, to include Arabic outlets such as Al-Jazeera. Ten percent of the U.S. reporters were to be selected from "local media that were from the towns where troops were coming from."[19] The military distributed assignments but allowed the news organizations to select their own reporters.

War coverage would not be limited to embedded reporters. News organizations could send non-embedded reporters, or "unilaterals," but Clarke emphasized that, due to the inherent dangers in combat, the safety of non-embedded reporters could not be guaranteed. In fact, unilaterals were discouraged from approaching the battlefield, as they or their vehicles could be misidentified as combatants.

Embed Ground Rules

DoD released a nine-page document detailing the ground rules to which the embed journalists had to agree in order to be assigned to a unit.

2. Policy
2.A. ... The Department of Defense (DOD) policy on media coverage of future military operations is that media will have long-term, minimally restrictive access to U.S. Air, Ground and Naval Forces through embedding. Media coverage of any future operation will, to a larger extent, shape public perception of the national security environment now and in the years ahead. ... We need to tell the factual story--good or bad--before others seed the media with disinformation and distortions, as they most certainly will continue to do. Our people in the field need to tell our story--only commanders can ensure the media get to the story alongside the troops.
2.C.3. Units should plan lift and logistical support to assist in moving media products to and from the battlefield so as to tell our story in a timely manner. In the event of commercial communications difficulties, media are authorized to file stories via expeditious military signal/communications capabilities.
3. Procedures
3.F. Embedded media operate as part of their assigned unit. An escort may be assigned at the discretion of the unit commander. The absence of a PA [public affairs] escort is not a reason to preclude media access to operations.
3.G. Commanders will ensure the media are provided with every opportunity to observe actual combat operations. The personal safety of correspondents is not a reason to preclude media access from combat areas.
3.Q. The standard for release of information should be to ask "Why not release?" [rather than] " Why release?" Decisions should be made ASAP, preferably in minutes, not hours.
3.S. Media will only be granted access to detainees...within the provisions of the Geneva Conventions of 1949.
4. Ground rules
4.A. All interviews with service members will be on the record. Security at the source is the policy. Interviews with pilots and aircrew members are authorized upon completion of missions; however, release of information must conform to these media ground rules.
4.C. Media embedded with U.S. Forces are not permitted to carry personal firearms.
4.G. The following categories of information are *not* releasable:
4.G.14. Information on effectiveness of enemy electronic warfare.
4.G.17. Information on effectiveness of enemy camouflage, cover, deception, targeting, direct and indirect fire, intelligence collection, or security measures.
4.G.18. No photographs or other visual media showing an enemy prisoner of war or detainee's recognizable face, nametag or other identifying feature or item may be taken.

TABLE 4-1: EXCERPTS FROM THE EMBED GROUND RULES

The document detailed a variety of responsibilities for the media as well as the military and "do's and don'ts" that defined the conditions for access and coverage. Table 4-1 is excerpted from the ground rules.

It was clear from the ground rules that the military intended to allow as much access, interaction, and coverage as possible while maintaining tight operational security.

Media Boot Camps

In an effort to familiarize reporters with the military and the possible conditions in which they would work, the military offered news organizations orientation training. Many reporters spent one week at one of the Pentagon's "Embed Boot Camps," where they "were given a crash course in all things military ..."[20] to include nuclear, biological, and chemical training and first aid. The boot camps were held at Fort Benning, Georgia; Fort Dix, New Jersey; and Quantico Marine Corp Base and Norfolk Naval Station in Virginia. The training was not required but encouraged. Reporters hoping to be selected for "choice" embed assignments hoped to improve their chances by participating in the boot camps. The training was designed to be educational and challenging. Andrew Jacobs, a *New York Times* prospective embed, termed the week as, "alternately enlightening, entertaining, horrifying, and physically exhausting."[21]

Training camps tested the mettle of embed hopefuls. The training "weeded out those who mistakenly thought that covering a war would be a heck of an adventure. After barely surviving pretend war, some opted to not experience the real thing."[22]

In addition to the boot camps, many reporters were given the opportunity to spend time with military units training in the U.S. prior to going off to war. This allowed the reporters and military to build trust in each other and to get familiar with each other's terminology and routines. It also allowed the news organizations and reporters the opportunity to test their new equipment, techniques, and procedures for reporting in what would be a fluid, hectic environment.

Walter Rogers of CNN noted, "that the U.S. Army was nothing short of brilliant in terms of the way they prepared us for it... you get to know the people you're covering... and you build a rapport. And that rapport stands you through the whole time very well."[23]

News Organizations Prepare For War

With the embed policy in place, journalists volunteering to go, and new-generation communication technology available to them, news organizations spent millions of dollars in ramping up to cover a war like never before. As with any costly, large-scale operation, proper planning and preparation by the news organizations was essential. There were a multitude of logistics questions and internal policy issues for which to plan and factor, which were not present in the previous war with Iraq.

Important questions included the following:

- What type of communications equipment and how much to bring?
- How do you get the equipment inside Iraq?
- What type of vehicles could be obtained and used?
- What type of safety equipment was needed?
- What would be the safest way to travel?
- Do we send unilaterals? If so, how many?

Factors to plan for included the following:

- Passports and visas,
- Food,
- Coordination between anchor desks, CENTCOM and the Pentagon,
- Utilization of on-air retired military for analysis,
- Injury or death of a reporter,
- Loss of equipment.

Planning for large-scale, fast-moving operations far from home is not common to news organizations, as it is to the military, so they had to learn fast and on-the-job.

Concerns Over The Embed Policy

Despite the tremendous momentum for both the military and the media in gaining access to cover battlefield operations live, the policy had many detractors from the outset. With the plan for the embedded journalists to live, eat, sleep, and do everything their military counterparts would do—except to carry arms—some questioned whether they would grow too "close to the military personnel with whom they are traveling" and "could sacrifice objectivity and a broad range of reporting in return for access."[24] These voices argued that embeds would be "in bed" with their military units. Dan Rather of CBS News quipped about the arrangement that, "there's a pretty fine line between being embedded and being entombed."[25]

Many countered this concern by noting the close working relationships of those who cover political campaigns or police beats and manage to maintain objectivity.

Other concerns related to possible censorship by the military. Critics speculated that the press might not be allowed to operate freely or film and report on what they desired, especially if the coverage was disturbing or unflattering to the military.

Of concern to all was the safety and security of the embedded journalists. Being "up close and personal" with front-line troops in the line of fire, and possible chemical attack, called for equipping crews with body armor, helmets, and gas masks. Corresponding training on the proper wear and use of the equipment became a necessity. Despite the precautions, the nightmare scenario of journalist vulnerability on the battlefield was realized.

COVERAGE DURING DECISIVE OPERATIONS (WAR)

The challenge facing news organizations was to provide an accurate depiction of war from a variety of angles and from numerous resources. In addition to the "embeds" and unilaterals, reporters were stationed on ships, at CENTCOM headquarters in Doha, Qatar, in Kuwait staging areas, and at the Pentagon. As reporters in the field covered only their "slice" of the war, the big picture of operations would have to be assembled at media headquarters by producers, anchors, and editors.

To aid in providing newsrooms, on-air anchors, and the public a better understanding of military operations, scores of retired military experts were hired. In the lead-up to the war, they assisted news organizations in developing briefing materials regarding the variety of military hardware and systems, as well as offering insights as to how the war might be fought. During the combat operations they were available for 24/7 analysis.

At the onset of combat operations, the television media utilized their state-of-the-art technology to provide captivating, real-time images of the battlefield: tanks speeding through the desert, firefights, and close air support. This riveting coverage fueled the public's thirst for information in a manner never before achievable. It was as if the public was drawn and glued to their televisions, like motorists staring at an accident scene.

U.S. broadcast networks and cable news outlets were on the air live twenty-four hours a day, displaying virtually all that the embeds could provide—from exciting confrontations with the enemy to mundane chores like shoveling foxholes. It was during these alternating events that the Pentagon claimed its largest public relations success—the display of American soldiers, marines, airmen, and sailors as everyday people in extraordinary circumstances who were dedicated to serving their country and protecting their buddies. These images of bravery and of camaraderie combined with the "shout outs" to family and friends back home were priceless in lifting the level of patriotism, appreciation, and support for the troops.

Shortly after combat operations commenced, it was clear that embedded journalists were the center of the coverage. Television reporters beamed back real-time visuals to the short-attention spanned, instant gratification, TV- and video game-nurtured viewer. Print journalists transmitted their fascinating, detailed accounts of the battlefield to traditional newspapers and Internet sites.

However, there were drawbacks to this new type of coverage, mainly with the amount and scope. Initially, there was a deluge of reporting. As Andy Rosenthal, managing editor of *The New York Times*, stated, "It's the Powell Doctrine of coverage—overwhelming force."[26] The torrent of information and reports coming into newsrooms proved challenging to those charged with assembling the big picture.

As anticipated, a "soda straw" effect emerged from the perspectives of the widely stationed embedded reporters. Some embeds covered raging firefights and others experienced no battles. Often, there would be conflicting reports on the same issue, such as the availability of food for the troops. There were reports of some units conserving their meals-ready-to-eat, or MRE's, by limiting troops to two meals a day rather than three. But other embeds, like retired Lieutenant Colonel Oliver North of Fox News Channel, reported no such shortage with his Marines. Conflicting reports led to questions regarding troop's speed of advance, operational pauses, logistics and supply chains, and the preparation and overall effectiveness of the war plan.

Often there were disconnects between the reports from journalists, CENTCOM briefings, and the Pentagon. After a few iterations of these disconnects, frustration developed when neither CENTCOM nor the Pentagon could not or would not confirm reports from reporters in the field. These situations became prominent during events that could place the military in a negative light, such as incidents of fratricide or the apparent bombing of Iraqi civilians. Often the reporters stationed at CENTCOM and the Pentagon pressed hard for answers to pointed questions about these incidents as well as the progress of the war versus the plan. The military-media relationship at these two venues appeared to be more adversarial. This was the complete opposite of the relationships that had been forged between the commanders, troops, and embedded journalists. The most heated exchanges between reporters and the military occurred away from the battlefield, where reporters demanded more than what they could see, hear, touch in order to report.

This "soda straw" effect also resulted in what Defense Secretary Rumsfeld termed media "mood swings" about the cyclical reporting of rapid troop movements and battle successes as opposed to aviation crashes, service member casualties, and apparent fratricide. By the fifth day of the war, criticism of war planning, tactics, and personnel strength were rampant from many segments of the media, including the retired military analysts in newsrooms. Matthew Rose and John J. Fialka, journalists for The *Wall Street Journal*, commented on the public mood in writing, "the overload of scenes and dispatches is delivering an illusion that each hour's installment adds up to total insight—whipsawing the pubic mood from highs to lows...."[27]

The mood swings were quite evident with the first images of U.S. prisoners of war and of their fallen, mutilated comrades transmitted by Al-Jazeera. Iraqi television displayed U.S. POWs being questioned about their jobs and purpose within the country. This act hit the U.S. military hard, as it was an apparent violation of the Geneva Conventions. There was outrage directed at both the Iraqi government for this display as well as at the U.S. government by those opposed to the war. It was not until the joyous images of the rescue of Private Jessica Lynch and the continuing rapid advancement of Army and Marines Corps units toward Baghdad that the public mood shifted upward. It was clear that the U.S. will was a center of gravity.

Though embed coverage was exciting, not all were satisfied with the journalistic standards. Criticism was leveled at the embedded journalists as a result of their apparent lack of reports critical of coalition forces. Allegations were that the embed reports were skewed in favor of the military and displayed imbalanced coverage. Reporters stationed forward at CENTCOM commented to briefers that there was a dearth of reporting on Iraqi casualties, either combatant or civilian. Iraqi state-run media or Arab media outlets had been running daily video of civilian casualties credited to errant bombs or attacks that CENTCOM could not readily confirm nor deny. CENTCOM briefers offered details of these incidents following full, detailed investigations, but detractors saw this as stonewalling to cover up unflattering incidents.

Embedded reporters traveling with the troops were unable to report on the Iraqi war crime claims. Neither embedded journalists with U.S. units nor unilaterals in Iraq had the range of access necessary to verify or repudiate such claims. Unilateral reporters who managed to remain in Baghdad or traveled within Iraq by other means were able to report on the bombed sites and the accusations. However, questions arose about their possible manipulation by Saddam's Ministry of Information. Were the unilaterals allowed to freely report on what they saw or were they being used as part of Saddam's information campaign? A blast at a Baghdad marketplace exemplified the coverage dilemma. Unilaterals there could not independently determine if it was caused by an errant U.S. bomb or by an Iraqi bomb planted to turn international opinion against the U.S. and the coalition.

Embed vs. Unilateral Coverage

Embedded and non-embedded reporters, in search of the "truth" of war, faced many challenges. Both took risks of personal harm, but the unilaterals did not have the protection of coalition forces. News organizations faced a dilemma over sending embeds or unilaterals: enjoy virtual freedom of reporting in a dangerous war zone with no assurance of safety or accept guidelines on reporting in return for improved access to the battlefield and additional safety. Unilaterals, indeed, undertook safety risks in providing their reports. There were fourteen journalists killed in the war, and the majority of those casualties were unilateral reporters.

Jon Donvan, an ABC unilateral news correspondent, said, "we go in to talk to the civilians, then we hear the Pentagon tell us that a lot of civilians are soldiers pretending to be civilians. We're prime hostage material."[28] During the early stages of the conflict, he and his team of six would enter Iraq only during the daytime hours and into sections under American control. He stated that he did not believe that his perspective of the war was better than that of the embedded journalists, "just a different one."[29] His charge from ABC news was to cover segments of the war with the Iraqi people to gain insight as to their aspirations for the future in light of the coalition action and promises.[30] Embedded reporters on the move with the fast-advancing troops could not be afforded this opportunity.

POST REGIME CHANGE COVERAGE

By April 8, 2003, with the fall of Baghdad imminent, many embedded reporters left their assignments in support units or units far from the front. They knew that the story and the visuals were in Baghdad and they quickly sought units that would be entering the capital city.

Shortly after the toppling of Saddam's statue in Paradise Square, signaling regime change but not an end to combat operations, the news organizations shifted course. ABC, CBS, and NBC returned to regular programming. Cable news outlets resumed airing commercials and stopped operating live 24/7. In light of the millions of dollars spent in preparing for and operating in Iraq, economics dictated that television resume income-generating operations.

With the major conflict apparently over, many embeds left their military units and stationed themselves in makeshift bureaus at the Palestine Hotel. From there, they reported on coalition efforts to restore services and rebuild infrastructure. This story soon was overtaken by the Iraqi's expressions about newfound freedom following years of oppression and depravity—the looting of government facilities. Other embeds returned to family, showers, and familiar food and offered retrospective reports of their war experiences.

With the loss of the majority of the embedded journalists, there was a distinct change in the tone and focus of coverage from Iraq. In contrast to the soldier-centric coverage in the major combat phase prior to entering Baghdad, the next phase of reporting targeted many aspects of Iraqi life, the capture of Ba'athist leaders, and insurgent attacks against coalition forces. There was little war coverage, despite the fact that there was still fighting ongoing in the northern region of the country.

As the weeks passed and the military transitioned to stability operations, the two primary categories of stories to cover were the efforts to restore services and rebuild the country and the challenges that the coalition faced: protests over the lack of services and security, increased crime, casualties due to roadside bombs, and sabotage of oil pipelines.

Despite hundreds of "good news" stories like soldiers providing food and rebuilding schools, media coverage quickly refocused on problems. "If it bleeds, it leads" stories became the norm during stability operations. With the loss of the embedded journalists, and no American-led, Iraqi-run television news outlet to cover the positive developments in Iraq, the information advantage enjoyed during combat operations eroded. Major General Thurman, who was stationed at the headquarters of the Combined Force Land Component Commander during the war, speaking as part of the "Reporters on the Ground" Conference at the U.S. Army War College in September, 2003, said that during stabilization operations, "we lost the information superiority edge in some manner with the departure of the media ... suddenly all of the positive stories you had with the embeds are to a degree less visible."[31] Moreover, the U.S. information campaign, which had dropped millions of leaflets to communicate directly with the Iraqi people, suffered greatly by not setting up local television with Arabic speaking correspondents to show the positive works by the coalition in the effort to "win the hearts and minds" of the Iraqi people.

EMBED POLICY AFTER ACTION REPORT

So what is the best description of the war reporting from the embedded reporters? Truthful? Fair? Accurate? Jingoistic? Unbiased? Pro-military? Anti-Iraqi? Was it more "infotainment" or substance? It is a matter of debate that most likely depends on one's pre-war perspective. Most likely, all of the adjectives applied in some part. What is known is that, due to the dazzling array of technology available to them, the embedded reporters offered coverage of combat operations like that of no other conflict .

In measuring success, the media and the military must examine their objectives and expectations prior to the war. The news organizations had hoped that the embedded journalists would deliver real-time reports of the battlefield close to the action with reasonable freedom to report as they pleased. The military had hoped for the same as part of their information campaign as well as to counter inaccurate reporting of the war by either the Iraqi Ministry of Information or news outlets with an anti-war or anti-coalition agenda. It is fair to state that each side achieved its aims, though not without controversy or obstacles.

Alicia Sheppard, in *Narrowing the Gap: Military, Media and the Iraq War,* sums up the success from the perspective of American public opinion. The public "gained a better comprehension of what the military does and of the sacrifices and hardships thousands of Americans make on a daily basis. And it renewed pride in the U.S. military."[32]

Sheppard credited the media: "They were able to broadcast live in the midst of a battle—an astounding feat. They saw and reported what was happening on the ground without censorship and without information being filtered through military briefers. And in the process, they got an education on today's military, which the press admitted they sorely needed."[33]

71

Factors Leading To Success

The military successes or outcomes in the Iraq war did not lead to an improved relationship between the military and the media. The groundwork was laid in the preparations for the upcoming conflict.

A major factor in the improving relationship was Victoria Clarke's development and selling of the embed plan to both her superiors and to the media. Allowing battlefield access to military commanders and troops to reporters from around the world on a large scale was unprecedented. This was an important first step in healing old wounds of media resentment regarding previous conflicts' restrictions.

With the policy in place, operational commanders were clear on DoD's position on media inclusion and participation. The next big step was in making the embed policy a major portion of the concept of operations. Commanders, senior and junior alike, were directed to support the embed policy and media plan. The shift in the military's perspective of the media from that of an adversary to an ally was central to the mission.

Another factor in the improved relationship was the preparation offered to media via "boot camps" and early embedding. A better media understanding of the units and missions, coupled with investments in building rapport, paid off for both media and the military due to greater respect for each other's roles.

Thorough preparation by the news organizations and the professionalism of the embedded journalists in their desire to cover battlefield operations accurately despite the military's ground rules cannot be discounted. With ground rules set, soldiers and "embeds" in place, and the missions of the military and media clear, working relationships took root. An example of such a relationship between an embedded journalist and a military commander was that of CNN's Walter Rogers and U.S. Army Lieutenant Colonel Terry Ferrell, a cavalry squadron commander. They met up in Kuwait and immediately worked on building a rapport based on cooperation and honesty. There would be no off-the-record discussions. There would be no need. By the time the orders were given to move into Iraq, their relationship was strong. Ferrell encouraged his troops to be as open with Mr. Rogers as he was. Additionally, Ferrell kept Rogers informed of the plan and daily operations. Rogers understood and respected operational security and guarded it as a soldier would. Ferrell admitted that, at times, he would "vent his frustrations about situations to Walter," with the knowledge that their confidential talks would not be reported.[34] Such confidences were unthinkable in Vietnam's later years.

Areas For Improvement

Though successful in many ways, there is room for improvement with the embed policy and execution. The improvements can be classified as logistical, procedural, and journalistic.

A major complaint from the media was the inability to drive their own specialized armored satellite vehicles into the theater. This forced the media to strip the equipment from their vehicles and squeeze them into the military's "humvees." This resulted in cramped quarters for troops and reporters alike.

Media representative would prefer ground rules with fewer restrictions. At after-action public affairs conferences held following major combat operations, media and military conferees recommended that improved and longer embed training would mitigate the need for some of the current restrictions.

Along journalistic lines, conferees at the U.S. Army War College's "Reporters on the Ground" conference held in September 2003, detailed media criticism on the coverage of the war as a whole:

- Inadequate coverage of the big picture—including disconnects between headquarters and the front
- Inadequate coverage from the Iraqi perspective
- Inadequate coverage of the non-U.S. and non-Iraqi perspectives
- Lack of questioning of leaders into the cause to go to war
- Apparent sanitization of the horrors of war—no images of casualties on either side as restricted by the ground rules.

Military conferees commented on improved media coverage in the stability operations phase. An observation at the conference was that the media left too soon following the President's declaration of an end to major combat operations. The departure of the majority of the media and the military's public affairs representatives left a void in reporting about many ongoing unit operations. After the fact, a conferee suggested that reporters be embedded with civil affairs units specifically to cover activities involving civilians.

POLICIES FOR FUTURE CONFLICTS

The future of war is not entirely clear. In a globalization scenario, the possibility of large armies going head-to-head is greatly reduced, if not, unlikely. Therefore, asymmetrical conflicts, such as the Global War on Terrorism, are more likely. Retired Army Major General Robert Scales, former Commandant of the U.S. Army War College, envisions that "future conflicts will be fought by smaller, less-conventional, more technical teams…[which are] more SOF-like."[35]

The modern military has been utilized increasingly in operations other than major combat. These operations are termed, Military Operations Other than War or (MOOTW). The U.S. scalable military of the 21st century will be employed in appropriately sized "packages" depending on the operational scenario. Table 4-2 shows the range of military options and a proposed level of media involvement. By using this chart, the military and the media can customize a scalable media plan for media personnel and resources depending on the nature and

Military Operations	U.S. Goals	Examples	Media Involvement
WAR	Fight and Win	• Large-scale Combat Operations • Small-scale combat operations	• Embedded and Unilateral reporters • Pool reporter(s)
MOOTW	Deter War and Promote Peace	• Peace Operations • Counter Terrorism • Show of Force • Raids/Strikes • NEO • Nation Assistance • Counterinsurgency	• Pool/Unilateral • Small Pool • Pool • Small Pool • Unilateral • Unilateral • Small Pool
MOOTW	Promote Peace and Support US Civil Authorities	• Freedom of Navigation • Counter-drug • Humanitarian Assistance • Protection of Shipping • US Civil Support	• Pool • Small Pool • Unilateral • Pool • Unilateral

TABLE 4-2: LEVEL OF MEDIA INVOLVEMENT FOR THE MILITARY'S OPERATIONAL SPECTRUM

size of the operation. The criteria for customizing a proper media plan would include the level of and nature of hostilities expected, operational security, security of reporters, and cooperation and support of host nation versus non-permissive entry.

An example of utilizing a scalable media plan is illustrated in comparing the two categories of war and MOOTW. In the decisive operations phase of a large-scale war, there would be a large number of troops of all branches of service from coalition countries over a vast area. Since the nature of major combat is hostile and fluid, the military should maintain a tight control over the battlefield in knowing the location of friendly forces, enemy forces, and media. The development of an embedded journalist media plan, as in OIF, would be appropriate for the efficiency of operations and for the safety of the journalists. Similarly, embedding a pool reporter or two with a unit during the stability operations phase, where forces are employed on a smaller scale in combat situations equally as dangerous as a major conflict, is advisable. Operations of this nature include combating insurgents, raids on high-value targets, and actions involving volatile situations or culturally sensitive locations. Embedding one or two pool journalists would allow for appropriate media coverage and reduce the risks to media personnel. Assignment of the journalist(s) can be made via pre-arranged schedule based on days of the month or by a particular week.

In MOOTW, the nature of the mission, size of the forces, area of operation, level of hostilities, host nation support, and media access will vary greatly. The first section under MOOTW in Table 4-2 shows the variety of missions involved. Though military operations may be smaller in scale, the military may not be able to control the area of operations such as in war. The media will be less likely to accept guidelines in these operations, although DoD should still offer access to units involved. Operational commanders can expect the media to operate independently of the military in covering peacekeeping operations, NEO, and nation assistance. Commanders should leverage the media during these operations, as they could depict American troops in a positive light in support of U.S policy.

However, DoD should insist on a small pool of reporters to accompany forces in peacemaking operations, raids, strikes, counterinsurgencies, and counter-terrorist operations involving increased operational security requirements and greater risks to forces and journalists. While a small group of journalists can accurately and credibly report on the scope of operations, a larger group of reporters covering these swiftly moving and potentially lethal operations can be a hindrance to the forces and can negatively influence the mission.

In the remaining segment of MOOTW in Table 4-2, the operations are less likely to involve hostilities and operational security. Again, DoD should offer and encourage media access to units throughout these operations. The limiting factor in these operations would be those involving Navy vessels, where space may be at a premium. Therefore, in freedom of navigation operations, counter-drug operations via the sea, and protection of shipping operations, pool reporters are recommended.

CONCLUSION

In the information age, with access to billions of people via worldwide 24-hour news outlets, the Internet, and a variety of traditional media, the significance of information as an element of national power is highlighted, particularly during times of crisis and war. Following the tragedies of September 11, 2001, the messages emanating from the U.S. government and that of our enemies and detractors have been diametrically opposed.

As a superpower, the United States can stand mightily against those who have harmed it or have aims to do so. But in the court of public opinion, might does not always mean right. Therefore, it is essential that informational power be utilized in support of our national policies and actions.

The primary goals of the unprecedented access to the battlefield by the world's media via the embedded media policy were to demonstrate the professionalism of coalition troops and to counter disinformation by our adversaries. These goals were met.

Coalition troops, and especially the American soldier, sailor, airman, marine and Coast Guardsman, were portrayed by embedded journalists as fierce, efficient warriors as well as compassionate individuals. Reporting from embedded battlefield journalists countered disinformation generated by the Iraqi propaganda machine, as well as coverage from other outlets opposed to the campaign or to U.S. policies, and allowed the world to decide the truth for itself.

The strategy to achieve these goals was an unprecedented level of cooperation. The cooperation was initiated with the planning and preparation leading up to conflict and forged between the troops and journalists throughout the conflict. The cooperation fostered improved relationships between the media and the military. Each party benefited from the relationship and the coverage.

Can these same goals be met in future conflicts when there is less motivation toward cooperation, or when operations do not support embedding journalists? The conditions around future conflicts will certainly be different, and the relationship between the military and the media may have taken a new direction. Future conflicts will be covered by the media in some manner, with or without the full cooperation of the military. It is in the best interest of the military, in support of national policy, that a certain level of cooperation be maintained in order to leverage the media in shaping its messages and the images to be reported.

With the Global War on Terror, the continued threat of asymmetric warfare, and the transformation of the U.S. military to lighter, more rapid and capable, scalable forces, operational plans need to be developed to provide for the utilization and optimization of the media. These plans need to take into account the lessons learned from Operation Iraqi Freedom and need to allow for scalable media presence.

During OIF, critics leveled allegations that objective journalism suffered because of the close relationships that developed between the embedded journalists and their assigned units. The media will weigh that criticism and will not accept the same guidelines as in OIF. Issues that media organizations will push for in future conflicts include the following:

- increased independence of embedded journalists,
- roving embedded journalists,
- media-specialized vehicles for transmissions,
- media-contracted translators for covering opponents and local citizens.[36]

These issues will challenge the military in developing any future embedded journalist policy for major combat. They pose problems in the areas of the military's control over the area of operations, operational security, and the safety of journalists. Allowing journalists to roam from unit to unit is not recommended, as it will increase the likelihood of their injury due to combat fire or capture.

Allowing roving embedded journalists, in fact, may erode the basis for an improved relationship between the media and military troops: trust. By spending time with one unit, the journalists were able to develop trust with commanders and troops based on the esprit de corps developed by living and working together under the same conditions. U.S. commanders may be less trusting and less likely to share information with roving embedded journalists, which occurred with the unilateral journalists in OIF.

Media heads and Department of Defense personnel should continue to meet regularly to hammer out the issues presented. DoD should also encourage media embedding during scheduled military exercises in order to expose more journalists to a better understanding of the military as well as to highlight the military in transformation. Additionally, embedding journalists in exercises can act as a proving ground for new or improved media technology.

A forward look must also be given by the military concerning future conflicts that may strain the military-media relationship. The last two major conflicts have been won due to overwhelming power assembled against an over-matched opponent, with relatively few casualties compared to Vietnam and World War II. Future conflicts may bring mass casualties; journalists will have to report on this. A unit may be consumed by hostile fires or by an attack by chemical, biological or nuclear means; the images would be devastating to the American psyche. Even on a minor scale, the aftermath of reports unflattering to the military, such as American casualties, human rights violations, and civilian deaths, may again strain the relationship between the military and the media.

The military's goals in the future in working with the media should be the same as they were in OIF. The military and the media are dependent on each other, despite their rocky history. Flexibility in the future will be the key for each organization. Future strategic leaders must incorporate planning for media operations into U.S. information strategy. If we do not, our adversaries will. As the numbers of fallen forces increase, as more hostage videos are displayed and more insurgent attacks covered versus successful efforts to win "hearts and minds," the likelihood of erosion in U.S. public support increases. It is crucial that the good relationship built during Operation Iraqi Freedom continues to grow.

ENDNOTES

1. Thomas B. Rosensteil, Los Angeles Times: 22 November 1985, pg. 1 [database on-line]; available from ProQuest; accessed 19 October 2003.

2. David Jablonsky, "National Power," in U.S. Army War College Guide to Strategy, ed. Joseph R. Cerami and James F. Holcumb, Jr. (Carlisle Barracks, PA: Strategic Studies Institute, 2001), 98.

3. Walter Isaacson and Eason Jordan, "News from the Frontline," Wall Street Journal, Eastern edition, 6 January 2003, pg A.18. [database on-line]; available from ProQuest; accessed 29 September 2003.

4 .William V. Kennedy, "Roots of Conflict," in Media and the Military: Why the Press Cannot Be Trusted to Cover a War (Westport, CT: Praeger, 1993), 13.

5. Margaret H. Belknap, "The CNN Effect: Strategic Enabler or Operational Risk?" Parameters 32 (Autumn 2002): 103.

6. Ibid.

7. Kennedy, 89.

8. Alicia C. Shepard, Narrowing the Gap – Military, Media and the Iraq War (Chicago: McCormick Tribune Foundation, 2004), 19.

9. Howard Kurtz, Washington Post, Washington, DC., 28 April 2003, pg A01. Available from <http://www.washingtonpost.com/ac2/wp-dyn/A46401-2003Apr27>, Internet; accessed 18 October 2003.

10. Ibid.

11. Ibid.

12. Shepard, 19.

13. Ibid, 20.

14. Matthew Rose and Greg Jaffe, "Spinning War, Pentagon Aide Chalks Up Wins," Wall Street Journal, Eastern edition, 21 March 21 2003, pg B.1 [database on-line]; available from ProQuest; accessed 29 September 2003.

15. Shepard, 21.

16. Shepard, 10.

17. Ibid., 11.

18. Carol Kerr <carol.kerr@carlisle.army.mil>, "Your Media Paper," electronic mail message to Jose L. Rodriguez <jose.l.rodriguez5@us.army.mil>, 03 November 2003.

19. Bryan Whitman, "Interview with BBC TV," U.S. Department of

Defense Transcript, 18 April 2003. Available from <http://www.defenselink. mil/transcripts/2003/tr20030418-0142.html>, accessed 18 Oct 2003.

20 Andrew Jacobs, "My Week at Embed Boot Camp," New York Times Magazine, 2 March 2003, 34.

21 Ibid.

22. Shepard, 28.

23. Ibid., 30.

24. Joe Flint, "The Assault on Iraq: TV Brings 'Shock and Awe' Home -- For Now, at Least, Move to Embed Reporters Meets Goals of Pentagon, Networks," Wall Street Journal, 24 March 2003, pg A.13 [database on-line]; available from ProQuest; accessed 29 September 2003.

25. Associated Press, "Rather Expresses Doubts about War Coverage Plans," Los Angeles Times, 14 Feb 2003, pg E.40 [database on-line]; available from ProQuest; accessed 29 September 2003.

26. Jonathan Alter, "In Bed with the Pentagon," Newsweek, 10 March 2003, 45 [database on-line]; available on ProQuest, accessed 29 September 2003.

27. Matthew Rose and John J. Fialka, "War News: Even with More Play-by-Play, Truth Remains Elusive in Iraq," Wall Street Journal, 31 March 2003. pg A.1 [database on-line]; available from ProQuest; accessed 29 September 2003.

28. Mike McDaniel, "The Media: A different view of war," Houston Chronicle, 27 March 2003: pg A6 (589 words) [database on-line]; available on Lexis-Nexis, accessed 29 September 2003.

29. Ibid.

30. Ibid.

31. George D. Thurman Major General, US Army, briefing slides with scripted commentary about embedded media, Carlisle Barracks, PA, U.S. Army War College, 4 September 2003.

32. Shepard, 58.

33. Ibid., 59.

34. Terry Ferrell, Lieutenant Colonel, U.S. Army, interview by author, 10 March 2004, Carlisle Barracks, PA.

35. Robert H. Scales, Major General, U.S. Army (Ret), USAWC Public Affairs Conference, Carlisle Barracks, U.S. Army War College, 4 September 2003, videocassette.

36. Shepard, 75.

BIBLIOGRAPHY

Aukofer, Frank, and William P. Lawrence. *America's Team – The Odd Couple: A Report on the Relationship between the Media and the Military*. Nashville, TN: Freedom Forum First Amendment Center, 1995.

Belknap, Margaret H. "The CNN Effect: Strategic Enabler or Operational Risk?" *Parameters* 32 (Autumn 2002): 103-107.

Carruthers, Susan L. *The Media at War: Communication and Conflict in the Twentieth Century*. New York: St. Martin's Press, 2000.

Clarke, Victoria. "Public Affairs Guidance(PAG) on Embedding Media During Possible Future Operations/Deployments In The U.S. Central Commands (CENTCOM) Area Of Responsibility (AOR)," electronic message from Secretary of Defense for Public Affairs, 101900Z FEB 03.

Copeland, Peter. USAWC Embedded Media Conference. Carlisle Barracks: U.S. Army War College, 4 September 2003. Videocassette.

Ferrell, Terry, Lieutenant Colonel, U.S. Army. Interview by author, 10 March 2004, Carlisle Barracks, PA.

Flint, Joe. "The Assault on Iraq: TV Brings 'Shock and Awe' Home --- For Now, at Least, Move to Embed Reporters Meets Goals of Pentagon, Networks," *Wall Street Journal*, (Eastern edition) 24 March, 2003, A.13. Database online. Available from ProQuest. Accessed 29 September 2003.

Isaacson, Walter, and Eason Jordan. *Wall Street Journal*, (Eastern edition), 6 January, 2003, pg A.18. Database online. Available from ProQuest. Accessed 29 September 2003.

Jablonsky, David. "National Power." In *U.S. Army War College Guide to Strategy*, eds. Joseph R. Cerami and James F. Holcum, Jr., 87-106. Carlisle Barracks, PA: Strategic Studies Institute, 2001.

Jacobs, Andrew. "My Week at Embed Boot Camp." *New York Times Magazine*, 2 March 2003, 34-38.

Jones, Jeffrey. *Gallup Poll Tuesday Briefing*. 29 October, 2003. "Gallup Poll Analyses: Support for Iraq War Holds Steady at 54%." Available from http://www.gallup.com/poll/ releases/pr031029.asp?Version=p. Internet. Accessed 29 October 2003.

Kennedy, William V. "Roots of Conflict." In *Media and the Military: Why the Press Cannot Be Trusted to Cover a War*. Westport, CT: Praeger, 1993.

Kerr, Carol <carol.kerr@carlisle.army.mil>. "Your Media Paper." Electronic mail message to Jose L. Rodriguez <jose.l.rodriguez5@us.army.mil>. 3 November 2003.

Kerschbaumer, Ken. "The Rules of War." *Broadcasting & Cable.* 10 March 2003, 1. Database online. Available on ProQuest. Accessed 29 September 2003.

LaFleur, Jennifer. "Embed Program Worked, Broader War Coverage Lagged." *News Media and the Law,* Spring 2003, 4-6.

Nelson, Emily and Matthew Rose, "Media Reassess Risks to Reporters in Iraq." Wall Street Journal. (Eastern edition) 9 April, 2003: B.1

Nunez, Joseph R. "Lesson 15: National Security and the Media." In *Readings in War, National Security Policy, and Strategy.* Carlisle Barracks, U.S. Army War College, Department of National Security and Strategy. 2003. Vol. II.: 72-75.

Romano, Allison. "TV News Operations Modify Battle Plans." Broadcasting & Cable. 14 April 2003, 74. Database online. Available on ProQuest. Accessed 29 September 2003.

Rosensteil, Thomas B., *Los Angeles Times*: Nov 22, 1985, pg. 1; Database online. Available from ProQuest. Accessed 19 October 2003.

Scales, Robert H., Major General (Ret), USAWC Embedded Media Conference. Carlisle Barracks: U.S. Army War College, 4 September 2003. Videocassette.

Shepard, Alicia C. *Narrowing the Gap: Military, Media and the Iraq War.* Chicago, IL: Robert R. McCormick Tribune Foundation, 2004.

Smolkin, Rachel. "Media Mood Swings." *American Journalism Review.* Jun/Jul 2003, 16-20. Database online. Available on ProQuest. Accessed 24 September 2003.

Strupp, Joe. "Some Journalists Will Avoid Embed Checks." *Editor & Publisher.* 10 March 2003, 4. Database online. Available on ProQuest. Accessed 29 September 2003.

_____. "U.S. Military Trying to Make Peaces with Press." *Editor & Publisher.* 6 January, 2003: 45. Database online. Available on ProQuest. Accessed 29 September 2003.

Tebbel, John. *Media in America*: Newspapers, Books, Magazines, Broadcasting – How They Have Shaped our History and Culture. New York, N.Y.: Thomas Y. Crowell Company, 1974.

Thurman, George D. Major General, US Army, Briefing slides with scripted commentary. Carlisle Barracks: U.S. Army War College, 4 September 2003. Videocassette.

Trigoboff, Dan. "The Fight to get in the Fight." *Broadcasting & Cable*. 9 September 2002, 16-20.

Whitman, Bryan. "Interview with BBC TV." 18 April 2003. Available from <http://www.defenselink.mil/transcripts/2003/tr20030418-0142.html>. Internet. Accessed 18 October 2003.

Young, Peter, and Peter Jesser. *The Media and the Military: From the Crimea to Desert Strike*. New York: St. Martin's Press, 1997.

CHAPTER 5

LEVERAGING THE MEDIA: THE EMBEDDED MEDIA PROGRAM IN OPERATION IRAQI FREEDOM

Colonel Glenn T. Starnes
United States Marine Corps

"We need to tell the factual story—good and bad—before others seed the media with disinformation and distortion, as they most certainly will continue to do. Our people in the field need to tell our story—only commanders can ensure the media get to the story alongside the troops."

– Donald Rumsfeld

Margaret Belknap, writing in *Parameters* in 2002, commented, "The fourth estate [the media] offers a superb mechanism for strategic leaders and warfighters to transmit operational objectives and goals, as well as to reinforce policy objectives." Ms. Belknap stated that strategic leaders must be proactive in leveraging the media in order to inform audiences concerning objectives and end-states. She warned that if the military failed to leverage the media, they risked having the graphic images of war shown to the world and the American people in a distorted manner. Inaccurate or deceitful reporting of military actions could drastically affect the will and support of the American people, which is the strategic center of gravity for the United States. Loss of public support for a war could also affect the decision-making process at the strategic level.[1] Essentially, Ms. Belknap echoed the sentiment of many others who recommend that the military cease holding the press at arm's length. Instead, the military should embrace the press and leverage the media's technology and worldwide reach to further strategic goals.

SECRETARY RUMSFELD'S DECISION

During the build up to the war in Iraq, Secretary of Defense Donald Rumsfeld faced an important decision regarding the military's public affairs policy. He needed to decide the way in which the war would be covered by radio, television, and print media (hereafter referred to as the media). The Defense Secretary had three courses of action. He could continue the practice of limiting the media's access to the battlefield and simply conduct press briefings at the Pentagon and at the military's operational headquarters as done during Operation Enduring Freedom. Another option envisioned a return to the management of the media through the creation and use of media pools as had been done during Operation Desert Shield/Desert Storm, now known as Gulf War I. A third course of action suggested that the Department of Defense (DoD) and the military leverage the media using an extremely radical public affairs plan now referred to as the Embedded Media Program.

In consultation with his Assistant Secretary of Defense for Public Affairs, Victoria Clarke, Secretary Rumsfeld chose to implement the Embedded Media Program because he understood that the media coverage of the coming war would "shape public perception of the National Security Environment." The technology used by the media to report instantaneously from distant locations, along with the rise of non-American news agencies (specifically the Arab news agency, Al Jazeera), would overpower military public relations efforts. The American and international media had to have freedom of access and reporting, free of the restrictive nature of press pools and without unnecessary censorship. Secretary Rumsfeld announced his decision in his Public Affairs Guidance message dated 10 February 2003, "We need to tell the factual story— good or bad—before others seed the media with disinformation..."[2]

THE MEDIA AND THE MILITARY

While the concept of embedded reporters during war was not new, the number of reporters envisioned under the Embedded Media Program was much more robust than ever attempted in any previous conflict. Unfathomable to many strategic leaders was the fact that many of the reporters would be able to go 'live' from anywhere in the battlespace with news of battles, complete with audio and television images of death and destruction. Remembering the impact of edited and delayed film reports during the Vietnam War, several military leaders had difficulty trusting the media enough to allow unlimited access. The by-product would be brutal images of war and death—instantly televised to every American living room.

Much of the senior and career level leadership (officer and enlisted) of today's military remains scarred by Vietnam and its aftermath. A whole generation of military leaders believes that the United States lost the war in Vietnam because the media turned public opinion against the soldier in the field. This belief in a media betrayal shaped the military's view of the media and the ethics of reporters during the past two decades. Many Americans (both military and civilian) agree with the worries expressed by General Colin Powell during the planning for the first Gulf War. In 1990, he felt that instantaneous battlefield reporting via television would bring home the horrors of war, complete with graphic scenes of combat and death. Reporters and cameras recording every step in a prolonged offensive ground war would create disillusionment and anti-war sentiment at home. These fears led to the policy of press pools.[3]

To make the Embedded Media Program work, Secretary Rumsfeld had to first demonstrate that the press pools of the first Gulf War were not the optimum way to use the media in a war. While the military liked the coverage of Gulf War I, and the American public had been ecstatic with General Norman Schwarzkopf's briefings and aerial bomb footage, the media left the war saying "never again." Walter Cronkite, writing in February 1991, decried the military's control of the media coverage through the press pools and the monitoring of stories and interviews with the soldiers in the field. In his opinion, the military was attempting to hide something. Cronkite believed that if the ground war had lasted longer than a few weeks, this sense of hiding something would have led to a breakdown of popular support for the war.[4]

THE POWER OF INFORMATION

In 1991, Saddam Hussein controlled the media in Baghdad, using it as a propaganda tool to show the death and destruction caused by the coalition bombing. Secretary Rumsfeld understood that if the American-led coalition failed to leverage the media in the coming war, the enemy might win the information battle by using the media to their advantage.

Deputy Assistant Secretary of Defense for Public Affairs Bryan Whitman remarked that the control of information was a major objective of the American-led coalition in Operation Iraqi Freedom (OIF). The military needed to "take the offensive to achieve information dominance and to counter Iraqi lies." Under Secretary Rumsfeld's guidance, the military planners came to understand that the "robust coverage" envisioned in the Embedded Media Program could build and ensure domestic/international support for the war. [5]

Major General J.D. Thurman, the Operations Officer for the Coalition Forces Land Component Commander in OIF, remarked that the presence of the embedded reporters on the front lines and the reports they filed countered the Iraqi propaganda during the assault on Baghdad. While 'Comical Ali' or 'Baghdad Bob' (as the Iraqi Minister of Information, Mohammed Saeed al-Sahhaf, was known) continued to announce that the coalition forces were nowhere near Baghdad, embedded reporters simultaneously reported the crossing of bridges leading into the city, the taking of the international airport, and the seizure of key points throughout the city.[6] The noted writer and commentator, Joseph Nye, referred to the military's ability to leverage the media as the "weaponization of reporters." [7]

In a sense Mr. Nye is correct. During OIF, the military succeeded in leveraging the media as part of its information operations campaign. The Embedded Media Program was both a propaganda tool for the strategic war effort and an operational counter-propaganda asset. Many readers may cringe when the word "propaganda" is used to define the leveraging of the media. Propaganda is not a dirty word. It is loosely defined as using any form of communication to influence an intended audience via rational or emotional arguments and personal opinion. When applied to military situations, propaganda seeks to gain audience support of military objectives.[8]

In the past few years, the strategic leadership of the military has begun to realize that public affairs (and by extension, the media) have a role in information operations. The Concept for Information Operations sees the role of public affairs as "a timely flow of information to both external (public) and internal (government/military) audiences." Public affairs is a "perception management tool."[9] During OIF, the Embedded Media

Program assisted the military in achieving information superiority over the Iraqis without disinformation or deception. Embedded reporting assisted decision makers at the operational and strategic levels in achieving information superiority.[10]

BENEFITS OF THE EMBEDS

Willie And Joe

In Operation Iraqi Freedom, there were over 770 journalists embedded with coalition military forces, with over 550 positioned with ground forces. At the height of the conflict, these reporters generated over six thousand stories each week.[11] As a battalion commander in the conflict, I witnessed first hand the impact these reporters had on both the military and the people back home. My observations confirmed what Philip Knightley wrote on the effect of leveraging the media over a decade ago: "On the home front, information—news—is used to arouse the fighting spirit of the nation, to mobilize public opinion about the war, to suppress dissent and to steel the people for the sacrifices needed for victory."[12] Lieutenant General William Scott Wallace, commander of the U.S. Army V Corps during OIF, remarked that the embedded media told the story of the soldier to the Nation . Otherwise, it would not have been told. The stories filed by the embedded media gave the public something to hold onto at the "mom and pop" level. The embeds gave the people back home the "Willie & Joe" of OIF. [13]

Ensuring Public Support

Dan Rather of CBS News saw another benefit of the Embedded Media Program. As with all conflicts for the past fifty years, a small but vocal anti-war movement existed in the United States during OIF. Left to its own devices, this anti-war element could have become extremely vocal. The embed reports, carried 24 hours a day on the cable news channels and as lead stories within the standard news agencies, focused audiences on the fighting men and women and silenced or smothered national dissent. Everyone, regardless of their opinion on the war, developed a "sense of pride and admiration" for those fighting on the front lines.[14]

Max Boot, writing in *Foreign Affairs*, echoed Rather's observations with a slightly different spin. Saddam Hussein failed to turn public opinion against the coalition even though he waged a strong propaganda campaign using the Arab news agencies. His attempts to sway public support through televised images of U.S. prisoners of war and Iraqi civilian casualties, along with reports of coalition atrocities, were successfully countered by embedded media reports. These reports provided believable accounts of the "professionalism, heroism, and restraint" of coalition forces. The world listened, watched, and believed these reporters more than they believed Arab news reports.[15] If the embedded reporters had not been present, the propaganda war would have had a much different outcome.

True Image Of War

Joe Galloway, the award-winning war correspondent, commented during the "Reporters on the Ground" conference (held at the Army War College in Carlisle, Pennsylvania) that the Embedded Media Program allowed the men and women on the front lines to be the military's best spokesmen. Gulf War I was a "Nintendo War." Ninety percent of the coverage of the war originated from Riyadh and the Combatant Commander's Headquarters. This provided the American public a "false image of war." Operation Iraqi Freedom and the embedded reporters corrected that image of war.[16]

The embedded reporters brought more than their ability to report the war first hand through the eyes and voices of soldiers. They also commented knowledgeably on the ability of the U.S. forces to improvise and adjust when the tactical situation forced a modification to combat plans. The embeds had access to the original plans and were aware of the commander's intent. They also understood that no plan survives the first shot. In OIF, instead of criticizing the tactical situation as plans changed, the embeds knew the whole story and reported to the American public the brilliant modifications to tactical plans that allowed the military to continue the offensive.[12]

The Australian Prime Minister, John Howard, had a different viewpoint on the benefit of the Embedded Media Program. He felt many of the great conflicts of the past century might have been fought differently or ended more quickly if embedded reporters had been present on the battlefield and in the commanders' headquarters. The Prime Minister doubted "that public opinion in great democracies would have allowed [the wars to continue], if they had known the full measure and impact of the horrendous loss of life that occurred in those tragic battles...." [18]

Prime Minister Howard has a point. Embedded reporters brought the war into every living room in America. Their reporting held commanders accountable for their actions and leadership. The American public relished the reporting and fully supported the war. If the military leaders had been incompetent and had prosecuted a bloody, nonsensical war, the embedded reporting would have shown that incompetence and led either to a change in commanders and tactics or to an end to the war.

Leveraging For Intelligence Value

Maintaining the support of the public back home while countering the lies emanating from Baghdad was only one of the benefits of embedded reporters. Commanders in Iraq leveraged the media for intelligence value to achieve immediate success on the battlefield. During the fighting in East Baghdad, a CNN television crew provided live footage of an infantry battalion's movement into the city. The senior Marine commander, Lieutenant General James Conway, watched the live CNN coverage in his headquarters east of the city. He saw friendly Iraqi civilians on the streets and noted the absence of enemy forces. Acting on these real-time images, LtGen Conway immediately approved a request to let the advancing forces continue until they hit enemy defenses. Similar live feeds from other embeds convinced the general to modify his entire plan and speed up the attack. [19] CNN coverage, from the embedded reporters, enabled LtGen Conway to make his rapid assessment, change his plans, and speed up the assault on Baghdad.

Of course the enemy can also leverage the media for intelligence value. During the Battle for Nasiriyah in late March 2003, the Iraqis reinforced the irregular forces fighting in the city with additional Fedayeen forces based on the embedded reporting of the battle on 23 and 24 March 2003. [20] Clearly, gathering intelligence from media reports is a double-edged sword. Commanders at all levels must be aware that their words and actions will be reported and leveraged by all participants.

LOSING THE INFORMATION WAR

For all its successful efforts in leveraging the media to achieve information operations objectives during the combat phase of the war in Iraq, the military failed to follow up and ensure success during the stabilization phase of the war. With the fall of Baghdad and Saddam's regime, embedded reporters left the front and returned home to new stories. By the end of April 2003, less than forty embedded reporters remained in Iraq. With their departure, the military lost the ability to leverage the media. They no longer enjoyed information superiority. With the loss of the embeds, there were too few public affairs officers in the stabilization force to ensure the remaining reporters, now based in Baghdad hotels, covered the good-news stories (previously observed by embedded reporters). Charged with getting a story to lead the hourly news coverage, the reporters concentrated on sensational stories of ambushes and riots, looting, and sabotage, vice stories of schools opening, water or power restoration, and so on.[21]

IMPROVING FOR THE FUTURE

Unilaterals

If embedding is the future of wartime public affairs, the Department of Defense must act now to correct the problems identified during OIF. The military must decide how to deal with the reporters who will be present on the battlefield but not embedded with a particular unit. Many news agencies feel they lost the big picture of the war because their reporters did not have the freedom to move around on the battlefield or to stop for in-depth stories on a particular event. At the "Reporters on the Ground" conference, news editors indicated a desire to increase the number of unilateral reporters in the next conflict. (Unilaterals are non-embedded or free-ranging reporters traversing the battlespace on their own, seeking a story.) Military leaders dislike unilaterals because they do not follow the rules. They endanger themselves, expect support and safety from the military forces, and claim ill will if they are shut out of interviews or worse, shot at by attacking forces. One Marine general called the unilateral reporters "leeches [who] take food and water, then run off."[22]

During the "Reporters on the Ground" conference, a number of panel members spoke at length on how unilateral reporters create dangerous situations in a war zone. At times these free-ranging reporters might find themselves ahead of advancing forces and in the middle of a deadly firefight. If operating on their own, they might be mistaken for the enemy. In August 2003, a freelance cameraman died while covering an insurgent attack near an Iraqi prison. As coalition armor forces approached the prison to respond to the incident, the cameraman leapt from his civilian vehicle and brought his camera to his shoulder to film the engagement. From a distance, the cameraman's actions resembled those of an insurgent preparing to engage the armor force with a Rocket Propelled Grenade. The U.S. forces shot and killed the cameraman from long range because they felt threatened by his actions.

A Special Forces panel member at the conference related an incident from Operation Enduring Freedom further demonstrating the dangers of unilateral reporters. Terrorists, masquerading as unilateral reporters, were able to breech the external security of a northern tribal leader's encampment. Once the terrorists got close enough, they detonated a car bomb, killing the tribal leader and setting back the war effort. If editors and media organizations want to employ more unilaterals in the future, they must realize that the trust and cooperation the unilaterals receive will not be the same as reporters enjoy in the Embedded Media Program.[23]

The Rules

The Public Affairs Guidance (PAG), signed by Secretary Rumsfeld, contained over five pages of rules for the reporters and the military. Although extensive and detailed, these rules were not well known. At the tactical level, commanders and reporters used common sense to determine what could be reported and when a reporter could transmit or "go live." Joe Galloway commented that in Vietnam a single page of rules sufficed (essentially a commander's intent or concept for media relations). While technology has improved, the basics of combat reporting have not changed. Common sense should be the basis for rules for embedding reporters.[24]

The scope of this paper does not lend itself to suggesting a complete modification of the rules. I believe they could be combined or reduced.

One of the rules that should be changed concerns the embedding of local media (i.e., from the military unit's hometown). The PAG allowed a regional/local reporter to embed and cover the preparation and deployment of a unit from home station to its arrival in the war zone. After arrival in theater, the reporter was required to apply to the OASD(PA), Office of the Assistant Secretary of Defense (Public Affairs), to be assigned as a combat embedded reporter. Unfortunately, the regional/local reporter had very little chance of being assigned to the hometown unit he had followed from the United States.[25] Accommodations should be made to allow one regional/local reporter to embed with a hometown unit from preparation through redeployment. If the rule is modified, the decision on which regional/local reporter should be allowed to embed must remain with OASD(PA). Commanders should not be placed in the position of choosing among reporters when they are preparing to deploy or engage in combat.

Reporting And Responding To Casualties

The rules prohibited the embedded reporters from reporting the names of casualties and required that they refrain from filming casualties. However, the rules allowed the embeds to report when a unit was in contact or had fought a battle. They could report there had been casualties, and even detail the exact number of dead and wounded if they knew for certain from first-hand knowledge.[26] While this seems an appropriate approach to combat reporting, the real-time reporting of casualties in a unit caused a number of families at home to worry, waiting for the feared visit from a military casualty assistance call officer.

I understand the embedded reporters were simply doing their job. As long as they did not identify the casualties or breach operational security, the military could not censor their efforts. On the other hand, the military must acknowledge the speed of real-time reporting and video images of battle and improve its casualty notification process. There is no way to get ahead of the news of battle or the reporting of casualties in a particular unit. But the military's laborious notification process for death or injury did not work in OIF and will not suffice in the next war. It is a given that the families of those in combat will be sitting at home hanging on every word concerning their loved one's unit. They will laugh and cry at the good news stories and wait in fear when reports of combat and casualties mention their units. The military must leverage technology to speed up the process of reporting battlefield casualties. Without improvements in casualty reporting, the military risks the erosion of credibility.[27]

The News Cycle

Beyond the narrow rules in the PAG, and indeed beyond the scope of military public affairs officers, there is room for improvement in how editors and commentators respond to reports from their embedded reporters. Rachel Smolkin, writing in *American Journalism Review* commented that "the relentless news cycle and the drama of a war unfolding live on television spurred a crush of grandiose pronouncements just days into the fighting—too early for journalists to offer any true perspective." Ms. Smolkin cautioned that editors and news directors should guard against reading too much into a single day of stories. Too often during OIF, the "talking heads" in the studios jumped to conclusions that had to be reevaluated an hour later when a new report arrived or an old report was revised.[28] The lesson here is one that military leaders know well— "first reports are almost always wrong and always incomplete." For the Embedded Media Program to survive and be relevant, editors, news presenters, and commentators must learn to manage the news cycle and raise the threshold for news alerts. This is not something the military can teach. It remains the responsibility of the media and those who manage the media to learn this lesson and to improve their profession.

CRITICS

Many military leaders who were skeptical of the Embedded Media Program prior to OIF are now singing its praises. On the other hand, journalists and editors are less than unanimous in their praise of the program. Robert Jensen, writing in *Progressive*, called the Embedded Media Program a "failure of success" of journalism. The technology that allowed instantaneous reporting was a success. But the reporting was a failure because the embedded reporters were unable to inform. They failed to provide the fullest possible understanding of the "what, why and so what."[29]

Mr. Jensen and others feel the embedded reporters identified too closely with their military subjects. Critics of the program believe the embeds allowed themselves to be censored by allowing the military to control their movements and reporting. Since only good stories appeared, the critics reason the military prevented the embeds from telling the whole story. Additionally, these critics suggest that the military staged many of the historic events telecast live. The most referenced photo-op was the pulling down of Saddam Hussein's statue in Baghdad.[30] The military and the reporters who embedded with combat units deny any claims of censorship or staged photo-ops. Critics like Mr. Jensen seem to be living in the past, specifically the era following the Vietnam War when the military and the media were at opposite ends of every imaginable spectrum. Journalists of Mr. Jensen's cut are distrustful of the military and believe uniformed leaders practice lying and misinformation. These critics possess a misconception of wartime journalism.

Responding To The Critics

In the forward to CBS News's chronicle of the war in Iraq, Dan Rather defends the embedded reporters and the Embedded Media Program. Rather, who was a war correspondent in Vietnam, admits that wartime journalism cannot be expected to provide the full story of all that is happening on the battlefield. In war there is no time for reflection on how the events unfolding before the camera lens fit into world events. In most cases the reporter will be unable to provide a general context for the images. Wartime journalists can only provide "a first draft of history," incomplete and possibly wrong or misleading.[31]

As to the claims of censorship or letting reporters only see the good news stories, one must consider the source of the criticism. The embedded reporters have not criticized the program. Those media professionals who remember other conflicts know that censorship was very much alive and well in World War II and later. The openness of the military in OIF was far beyond anything ever experienced. As a battalion commander with embedded reporters, and having talked to many other reporters, not one reporter mentioned a time when the content of his stories had to be cleared or "OK'd" by the military.

Need For A Strategic Analysis

One criticism of the Embedded Media Program that is valid and needs to be addressed by the Department of Defense concerns a lack of strategic reporting and analysis. The embeds provided tactical play-by-play. Their daily or hourly reports reflected the ebb and flow of the operation. Without someone at the Pentagon to put these reports into a strategic context, the media turned inward to poorly informed studio presenters or retired military officers from a past generation. Tactical stories of long supply lines and halted forces were taken out of context and turned into a bad news story. That bad news story was then fanned into a wildfire in a matter of hours.[32]

Consider LTG Wallace's comments on 27 March 2003. In response to a question from an embedded reporter, the V Corps commander commented, "The enemy we're fighting is a bit different than the one we war-gamed against." The *Washington Post* ran the story with Wallace's comments but deleted the word 'bit' from the quote. Television news presenters and military experts began talking about the war going badly based on the general's words. These discussions fed a media frenzy and created doubt with the American public concerning the military operations in Iraq. The Bush administration was seen as hiding the truth about the war. Much of this doubt began from a truthful story with an incorrect quote.[33] Even worse was the response from the Pentagon. Instead of providing an overlying strategic context to the Corps commander's tactical analysis, the Pentagon sought to downplay the comments and appeared to refute the commander on the ground.

An article in *USA Today* commented that the Pentagon must stop providing perspective (another word for "spin") and instead provide a strategic context to the Pentagon reporters. By providing the strategic context, the Pentagon could counter the current American penchant for "fast-forward thinking." The embeds gave the American public "Victory on Fast Forward." The "euphoria of liberating Baghdad" lasted eight hours, or one day's news cycle. Then the public and the studio-based presenters back in the states started clamoring for something new. The military had not completed the liberation of Baghdad before the public was asking for a redeployment and "Welcome Home" parades. Knowledgeable spokesmen working for the major news agencies conveniently based in the Pentagon could have proactively countered this "fast-forward mentality" by offering a strategic context for the actions being reported by the embedded reporters.[34]

A FINAL DISTURBING THOUGHT

There exists one disturbing aspect of the embedded reporting experiment. Is it healthy for a tactical commander's decisions to be affected by how the outcome of his actions will be reported in the news? It is well understood that the Pentagon wanted to leverage the media as part of its information operations campaign, but should tactical commanders become worried about how their actions might influence information operations?

David Zucchino, writing for *The Los Angeles Times,* told of how the commanding officer of 2nd Brigade, 3rd Infantry Division made a critical decision during the battle for Baghdad based on his ability to affect information operations through the reporting of his embedded reporters. On 7 April 2003, Colonel David Perkins, commander of the 2d Brigade, received orders to conduct a reconnaissance in force from the international airport into the heart of Baghdad to "test the city's defenses, destroy as many Iraqi forces as possible, and then come out to prepare for the siege of the capital."

U.S. forces had previously seized the airport and were continuing to engage targets throughout the city. Colonel Perkins had heard news reports of the Iraqi Minister of Information declaring the Iraqi forces were winning in the city, even claiming that Iraqi forces were in possession of the airport. Perkins wanted not just to attack the city, but also to stay there. He knew the attack would be reported live by his embedded reporters and thus counter Iraqi propaganda. The brigade's attack drove deep into downtown Baghdad, ending with the capture of one of Saddam Hussein's palaces. Once the attack was over, Colonel Perkins along with two of his battalion commanders participated in live interviews with an embedded Fox TV news crew. The brigade commander's decision and actions appeared to be working until he received word that his brigade headquarters (at the airport) had been hit by missile fire. Simultaneously, Colonel Perkins learned his supply line was in danger of being cut off and overrun.

Without a command post to serve as the brigade's command and control nerve center and a supply line to refuel and rearm the force, the brigade could possibly become trapped in the city and overrun. As Mr Zucchino writes, "Perkins knew the prudent move was to pull out ..." He had no reserves and no hope of immediate resupply. But Colonel

Perkins also knew that pulling out would validate the Iraqi propaganda lies. Trusting in his soldiers' ability to overcome the enemy attacks and keep the supply line open, the brigade commander elected to stay in the city. His decision proved to be the right one. His command center was able to recover, and the supply line defense held.[35]

Regardless of the outcome, the real question is whether Colonel Perkins made his decision based on the tactical situation or on how his brigade's actions would be reported? If the embeds had not been present on the mission to telecast the brigade's actions, what benefit would have there been in staying at the palace? He had achieved the division commander's objective by conducting the reconnaissance in force. His command was in danger, yet he elected to affect information operations through the media, vice conservatively fighting the tactical battle. Colonel Perkins's actions demonstrated initiative and fearless nerve, but I am concerned that his decision process was corrupted by the presence of the embedded reporters.

If my concern is founded in truth, senior leadership must recognize that embedded media will invariably affect the decision process of battlefield leaders. Media training for officers and senior enlisted must become an integral part of the training syllabus at all levels of military schooling. As part of tactical exercises, military leaders need to study and critique possible situations involving media reporting and their effect on operations.

Conclusion: Embedded Media—here To Stay?

Using the hindsight we all possess, it is hard to understand why it took so long for the Department of Defense to adopt the Embedded Media Program. Following Operation Urgent Fury (Grenada) in 1983, the 20th Century Fund Task Force on the Military and the Media found that "[the] free press, when it accompanies the nation's soldiers into battle, performs a unique role. It serves as eyewitness, it forges a bond between citizen and soldier. It also provides one of the checks and balances that sustains the confidence of the American people in their political system and armed forces."[36] Military leaders will resoundingly deny any need for the media to be watchdogs. What is lost on the military leader is that the American public has become all too familiar with its leaders requiring checks and balances. If the presence of the media within units in combat at all levels ensures the trust of the American public and strengthens their support, the military should look for ways to further improve the Embedded Media Program for the future.

At the "Reporters on the Ground" conference, a reporter asked whether embedding would be the standard public affairs policy for the future. The Pentagon officials at the conference avoided a definitive response, saying that the situation will dictate the policy. Phil Nesbitt, a media consultant, commented that embedding would have to be the future policy. "The genie is well out of the bottle."[37] I agree with Mr. Nesbitt. The American public wants reality TV. Instant battlefield reporting will be expected. If the military tried to fight a war without embeds, the claims of cover-up and deceit would once again rule the airwaves.

In August 2003, the military experienced a sample of the potential backlash and suspicion arising from a failure to employ the Embedded Media Program in a future conflict. By the end of Phase III Operations, the Embedded Media Program had become an integral part of the military's public affairs policy. Even with the departure of most of the embedded journalists, the few that remained with the deployed forces continued to enjoy a level of access to operations never before imagined by the military or the media. Relations between commanders and reporters were at an all-time high, and the military was continuing to reap the benefit of embedded reporting. Then, in mid-August, the Coalition Joint Task Force in Baghdad directed all commanders to deny reporters, photographers, and television crews access to "some" operations. The directive was a "significant shift" in the relations between the media and the military. Confusion reigned for a short time, as it appeared that operational security had won out over information operations. The directive was quickly rescinded, but the damage was done.[38]

Since the beginning of Phase IV, Stabilization Operations, the relationship between the military and the media has worsened. There are fewer embedded reporters and more unilaterals. The reporters feel they need the freedom to move throughout the city and country to get to the action. The military believes that only the bad news stories are getting told. Every reporter at the "Reporters on the Ground" conference admitted that they believe the military is hiding something or conducting a cover-up anytime the Pentagon announces that an incident "is under investigation." Distrust between the media and the military can easily be rekindled. The media will expect the Embedded Media Program to be employed every time America goes to war. The military will need to employ the program if they are to win the public affairs battle and the information operations campaign.

It is clear that Secretary Rumsfeld made the right decision regarding public affairs policy in Operation Iraqi Freedom. The Embedded Media Program was a resounding success for both the military and the American people. The military and the media overcame many barriers of distrust and antagonism. The task before us is to build upon the successes enjoyed in OIF and attempt to correct or minimize the problem areas. While the Pentagon might claim that each future conflict will have to be examined before determining a public affairs policy, the truth is that the "fork in the road" is behind us, and there is no turning back. The Embedded Media Program is here to stay.

ENDNOTES

1. Margaret H. Belknap, "The CNN Effect: Strategic Enabler or Operational Risk," *Parameters*, 32 (Autumn 2002), 110.

2. Secretary of Defense Message, "Public Affairs Guidance (PAG) on Embedding Media During Possible Future Operations/Deployments in the U.S. Central Command (CENTCOM) Area of Responsibility (AOR)," Washington, D.C. 101900Z February 2003; and Justin Ewers, "Is the New News Good News?" *U. S. News and World Report*, 134 (7 April 2003) [database on-line]; available from H. W. Wilson; accessed 23 September 2003.

3. Bob Woodward, *The Commanders*, (New York: Simon and Schustler, 1991), 315.

4. Phillip M. Taylor, *War and the Media: Propaganda and Persuasion in the Gulf War*, (Manchester, U.K.: Manchester University Press, 1992), 273. Cronkite was a battlefield reporter in World War II as well as Vietnam, his ideas of press pools are most likely shaped from his own experiences.

5. John Cook, "Military, Media Meet Off Battlefield to Debate War Coverage," *Chicago Tribune*, 18 August 2003.

6. Katherine M. Skiba, "Journalists Embodied Realities of the Iraq War," *Milwaukee Journal Sentinel*, 14 September 2003.

7. Joseph S. Nye, Jr., "U.S. Power and Strategy After Iraq," *Foreign Affairs* 82 no.4 (July/August 2003), 67.

8. W. C. Garrison, "Information Operations and Counter-Propaganda: Making a Weapon of Public Affairs," Strategy Research Project (Carlisle Barracks: U.S. Army War College, 17 March 1999), 4-5.

9. U.S. Army War College, "Information Operations Primer," Department of Military Strategy, Planning and Operations (Carlisle Barracks: U.S. Army War College, January 2001), 48.

10. Ibid., 2. Information superiority is defined as the collection, processing and dissemination of information without interruption or interference while at the same time exploiting or denying the enemy the ability to do the same.

11. Skiba.

12. Taylor, 18-19.

13. Gathered from notes taken at a conference conducted by the Center for Strategic Leadership at the U.S. Army War College, "Reporters on the Ground," held 3-5 September 2003 at Carlisle Barracks. Willie and Joe are famous cartoon characters of World War II depicting the average American 'dog-face' soldier on the European war front.

14. Dan Rather, *America at War: The Battle for Iraq: A View From the Frontlines*, CBS News (New York: Simon and Schustler, 2003), ix.

15. Max Boot, "The New American Way of War," *Foreign Affairs* 82 no. 4 (July/August 2003), 54.

16. Skiba.

17. Boot, 55.

18. "Embedded Media 'Shorten Wars'," News.com.au, [journal on-line]; available from http://www.news.com.au/common/printpage/06093,6260149,0 0.html internet; accessed 23 September 2003.

19. Bing West and Ray L. Smith, *The March Up: Taking Baghdad with the 1st Marine Division*, (New York: Bantam Doubleday Dell, 2003), 226-227. The Battle for Tikrit (described on page 251) affords another example of leveraging the media for intelligence value. Brigadier General John Kelly commanded Task Force Tripoli whose mission was to capture Saddam's hometown following the fall of Baghdad. As his task force approached the town, BGen Kelly called up the reporters embedded with his unit along with some local Iraqi tribal leaders. He told them to spread the word that the Marines were here, and that anyone threatening the life or property of another individual (Iraqi or American) would be dealt with - with deadly force. The word was dispersed via the news and word of mouth that afternoon and evening. By the next morning the Kurds who had planned to attack the town had withdrawn and the town quickly surrendered to the Marines.

20. Ibid., 48.

21. Skiba.

22. Cook.

23. Reporters on the Ground conference.

24. Ibid.

25. Secretary of Defense, "Public Affairs Guidance."

26. Ibid.

27. Robert S. Pritchard, "The Pentagon is Fighting – and Winning – the Public Relations War," *USA Today* (July 2003) [database on-line]; available from H.W. Wilson; accessed 23 September 2003.

28. Rachel Smolkin, "Media Mood Swings," *American Journalism Review* (June/July 2003) [database on-line]; available from Infotrac; accessed 23 September 2003.

29. Robert Jensen, "The Military's Media," *Progressive* 67 (May 2003)[database on-line]; available from EBSCO Host; accessed 23 September 2003.

30. *USA Today*, Ewers; and Jensen.

31. Rather, xii. Philip Taylor, writing about war and the media in the 1990's (page 12 of his book, *War and the Media*), supported the concept of war correspondents being neither all seeing nor all knowing. Journalists in war "chronicle only what they see ... even their judgment of what is important is determined by the same sort of experience, perception, education, even emotions, that effect all human beings."

32. Smolkin.

33. Boot, 48.

34. Pritchard. Brigadier General Vincent Brooks said much the same thing during the "Reporters on the Ground" conference. It was not the job of the commanders or reporters at the tactical and operational level to provide a strategic context for OIF operations. That duty fell to Defense Department personnel in the Pentagon. The fact that the Pentagon failed to provide that strategic context and instead let the analysts in studios fill in the strategic 'holes' needs to be rectified for all future conflicts.

35. David Zucchino, "Thunder Run," *Los Angeles Times*, 7 December 2003.

36. John J. Fialka, *Hotel Warriors: Covering the Gulf War,* (Baltimore, Maryland: The Woodrow Wilson Center Press, 1991), xiv.

37. Skiba.

38. Stephen R. Hurst, "New Restrictions for Embedded Media Imposed, Then Rescinded," Associated Press, *Air Force Times*, (14 August 2003).

BIBLIOGRAPHY

Aukofer, Frank and William P. Lawrence. *America's Team: The Odd Couple – A Report on the Relationship Between the Media and the Military.* Nashville, Tennessee: The Freedom Forum First Amendment Center, Vanderbilt University. 1995

Belknap, Margaret H. "The CNN Effect: Strategic Enabler or Operational Risk?" *Parameters*, 32 (Autumn 2002): 100-112.

Boot, Max. "The New American Way of War." *Foreign Affairs* 82 no. 4 (July/August 2003) 41-58.

Burnett, John. ""Embedded/Unembedded II." *Columbia Journalism Review* 42 (May/June 2003) Database on-line. Available from H W Wilson, Accessed 23 September 2003.

Chessman, Curtis P. "Information Operations–Harnessing the Power." Strategy Research Project. Carlisle Barracks: U.S. Army War College, 8 April 2002.

Cook, John. "Military, Media Meet Off Battlefield to Debate War Coverage." *Chicago Tribune,* 18 August 2003.

"Embedded Media 'Shorten Wars'." News.com.au. Journal on-line. Available from http://www.news.com.au/common/printpage/0,6093,6260149,00. html Internet. Accessed 23 September 2003.

Ewers, Justin. "Is the New News Good News?" *U.S. News and World Report* (7 April 2003) 134 Database on-line. Available from H W Wilson, Accessed 23 September 2003.

Fialka, John J. *Hotel Warriors: Covering the Gulf War.* Baltimore, Maryland: The Woodrow Wilson Center Press, 1991.

Garrison, W.C. "Information Operations and Counter-Propaganda: Making a Weapon of Public Affairs." Strategy Research Project. Carlisle Barracks: U.S. Army War College, 17 March 1999.

Hews Stephen and Marvin Kalb, eds. *The Media and the War on Terrorism.* Washington, D.C.: Brookings Institute Press, 2003.

Hoffman, David. "Beyond Public Diplomacy." *Foreign Affairs* 81 (March/April 2002) 83-95.

Hurst, Stephen R. "New Restrictions for Embedded Media Imposed, Then Rescinded." Associated Press, *Air Force Times*, 14 August 2003.

Jensen, Robert. "The Military's Media." *Progressive* 67 (May 2003) Database on-line. Available from EBSCO Host, Accessed 23 September 2003.

Nye, Joseph S. Jr. "U.S. Power and Strategy After Iraq." *Foreign Affairs* 82 no. 4 (July/August 2003) 60-73.

Pritchard, Robert S. "The Pentagon is Fighting-and Winning-the Public Relations War." *USA Today* (July 2003) Database on-line. Available from H W Wilson. Accessed 23 September 2003.

Rather, Dan. America at War: *The Battle for Iraq: A View from the Frontlines*. CBS News. New York: Simon and Schustler, 2003.

"Reporters on the Ground," A Center for Strategic Leadership Conference conducted at Carlisle Barracks: U.S. Army War College. Notes taken by author, as a panelist 3–5 September 2003. All statements and opinions expressed during the entire conference were on the record.

Secretary of Defense Message, "Public Affairs Guidance (PAG) on Embedding Media During Possible Future Operations/Deployments in the U.S. Central Command (CENTCOM) Area of Responsibility (AOR)," Washington, D.C. 101900Z February 2003.

Skiba, Katherine M. "Journalists Embodied Realities of the Iraq War." *Milwaukee Journal Sentinel*, 14 September 2003.

Smolkin, Rachel. "Media Mood Swings." *American Journalism Review*, (June-July 2003) Database on-line. Available from Infotrac. Accessed 23 September 2003.

Taylor, Phillip M. *War and the Media: Propaganda and Persuasion in the Gulf War*. Manchester, U.K.: Manchester University Press, 1992.

U.S. Army War College. "Information Operations Primer." Department of Military Strategy, Planning and Operations. Carlisle Barracks: U.S. Army War College, January 2001.

West, Bing and Ray L. Smith. The March Up: Taking Baghdad with the 1st Marine Division. New York: Bantam Doubleday Dell, 2003.

Woodward, Bob. The Commanders. New York: Simon and Schustler, 1991.

Zucchino, David. "Thunder Run." Los Angeles Times, 7 December 2003.

www.ingramcontent.com/pod-product-compliance
Lightning Source LLC
Chambersburg PA
CBHW072208280526
45788CB00002B/925